CONTEMPORARY RAGTIME GUITAR

Stefan Grossman

Oak Publications · New York
Music Sales Limited · London

PHOTOGRAPHS

Book design by Jean Hammons and Tara Collins

© 1972 Oak Publications
A Division of Embassy Music Corporation
24 East 22nd Street, New York, NY 10010 USA

Music Sales Limited
8/9 Frith Street, London W1V 5TZ England

Music Sales (Pty.) Limited
120 Rothschild Street, Rosebery, Sydney, NSW 2018, Australia

Library of Congress Catalogue Card Number 77-170117
International Standard Book Number 0-8256-0130-4

Contents

Dedicated to Harry Smith

". . . It doesn't sound like a good thing to do: start at the beginning and work forward. You don't want to work backwards?"

Introduction

You can't help but develop your own guitar style. The sound that you produce will be unique to you. Your fingers, your mind and even the make of instrument you play are all factors that will contribute to a new sound that can only be classified as yours. No matter how hard you might try to imitate another guitarist you can never lose your own sound.

There are many paths to follow in learning about the guitar. I was taught a great deal by old songsters and bluesmen. Mississippi John Hurt, Son House, Skip James, Fred McDowell and Reverend Gary Davis all showed me a world of music and a way of life I had never seen. My relationship with these old bluesmen paved the foundation for my knowledge of country blues guitar techniques. These are documented in my five volume series at Oak.

At the same time that I was studying country blues, I was also very involved with friends in arranging and composing new tunes. I was lucky to be surrounded by so many excellent young guitarists. Every year I saw my style develop and watched the styles of my friends change too. We were more concerned with growth than with discussing the meanings and function of a song. We never really understood the theory behind a piece of music but we learned to play what we heard. We were never too concerned with playing the exact melody of a song. We respected the freedom to add and subtract from the songs we played and this put us into a world labeled "the folk process".

This is the first in a series of books that will document the changes that took place during this period, a period that is in fact not yet over. This is also an instruction book. By studying it you will be able to learn modern *unorthodox* guitar techniques that have been developed. It is not for the beginner but geared more for the player who knows a few chords and understands what he wants to learn. The tunes presented in this book are in order of increasing difficulty. I have chosen a wide range of pieces in hopes that you will broaden your musical knowledge.

This book pulls together various loose ends. It begins with some original blues compositions, very much an extension from my *Country Blues Guitar Series*. It then delves into the art of arranging fiddle tunes, ragtime songs and classic piano rags to the guitar. This will show you a world of tunings and chord positions that you would never encounter in an ordinary method of guitar teaching. The last section is a glimpse into what all this might lead to. The foundation for *Contemporary Ragtime Guitar* has been traditional music. The subsequent volumes in this series will deal with music not so firmly rooted in past sounds. The last section of this book is only a hint of what will follow.

I would like to stress the importance of the listening process. This teaching method depends greatly on you, the reader. I hope that you will endeavor to listen to the records or tapes that are listed before each selection. This will help you considerably in grasping the hidden musical message behind the printed page.

The approach presented in this volume is exciting because there are no rules. Good music and guitar playing can only be hindered by rules and methods. I hope that this book will show you a new world for hearing and playing guitar.

Dave Laibman, Marc Silber, Aurora Block, Steve Mann, John Fahey, Ry Cooder, Ric Schoenberg, Eric Kaz, Bert Jansch, Davy Graham and Martin Carthy have all provided me with wonderful songs and compositions that will full up many volumes before the story of contemporary guitar techniques has been told.

I would like to thank Herbert Grossman, Jack Prelutsky and Christine Brown for the use of their photographs.

I hope that you will enjoy this study and that it will contribute positively to your musical development.

Contemporary Blues

Little Rock Blues Number Two

This arrangement was put together in 1966, when I was staying in Mecker, Colorado. It shows the strong influence of a piece called *Little Rock Blues* sung by Pearl Dickson. On this old *race* record of the twenties there are two guitars playing behind the singer. I was very intrigued by their accompaniment as it had a distinct feel very different from the many blues I knew recorded by Blind Boy Fuller, Blind Blake or Big Bill Broonzy.

I thought it would be interesting to try putting both guitar parts into one. At first this proved very difficult as the counterpoint runs that would have been necessary to duplicate their sound exactly were physically impossible to play on one instrument. So after much trial and error I came up with what I called *Little Rock Blues Number Two*.

It begins somewhat like the original with a high treble run being played against a steady alternating bass. But once this is completed the guitar playing jumps from style to style as frequently as the song changes chords. The piece is played in the key of G. When the song modulates to the C chord, the playing changes first to an old Memphis sound (reminiscent of Frank Stokes) and then to a more modern *white* city approach of playing a blues tune. In the last section the style is very similar to that shown to me by a great Los Angeles guitarist named Steve Mann. Here the guitar keeps its own sound yet imitates the piano. Several counterpoint runs are played but more to emphasize the rhythm than to stress two separate lines.

It might be interesting for you to compare different styles of playing a blues tune in the key of G. I suggest you look at the transcriptions for the following songs found in my various other Oak instruction volumes.

Shake That Thing by Mississippi John Hurt (*Country Blues Guitar*)
Where Is My Good Man by Memphis Minnie (*Country Blues Guitar*)
Ragged and Dirty by Willie Brown (*Delta Blues Guitar*)
Whiskey Head Blues by Tommy McClennan (*Delta Blues Guitar*)
Policy Blues by Blind Blake (*Ragtime Blues Guitarists*)

Try to hear the original *Little Rock Blues* by Pearl Dickson that can be found on the re-issue record *Country Girls (Origin of Jazz Library)*. I have recorded my arrangement on *The Gramercy Park Sheik* (Kicking Mule Records, Sonet Records).

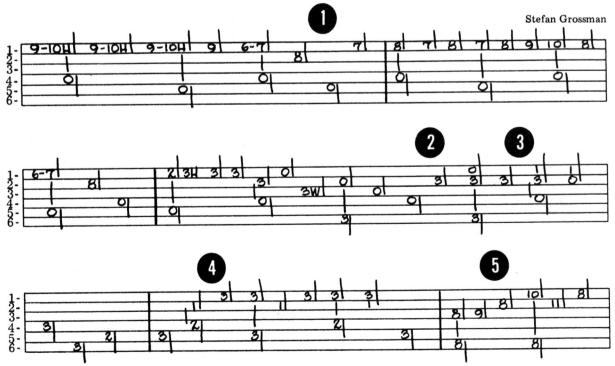

Stefan Grossman

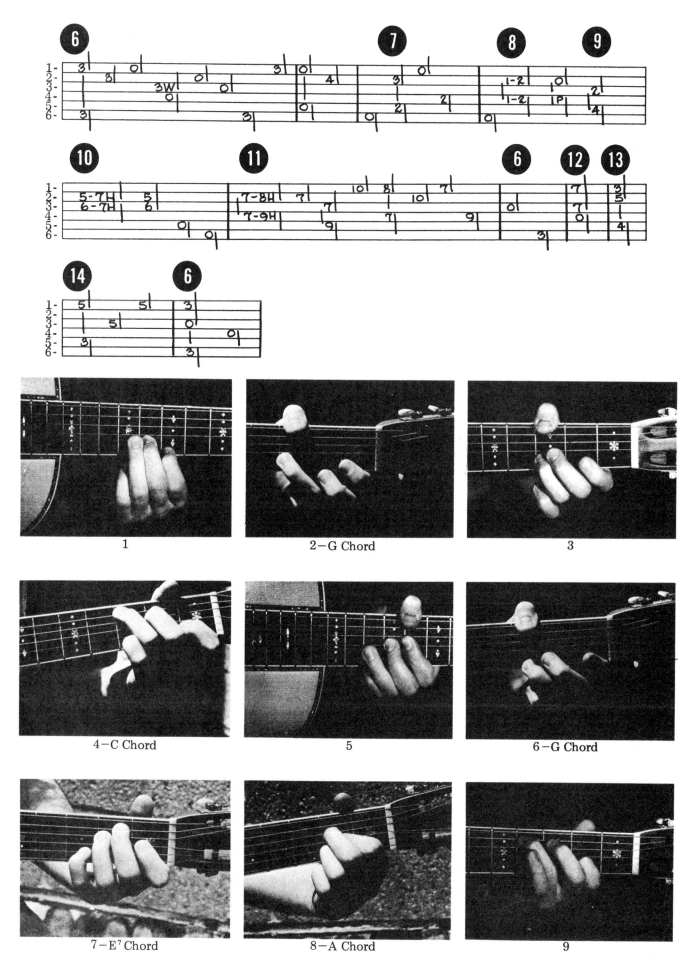

1

2 – G Chord

3

4 – C Chord

5

6 – G Chord

7 – E⁷ Chord

8 – A Chord

9

9

Little Rock Blues Number Two

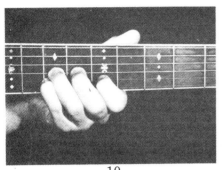
10

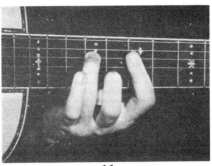
11

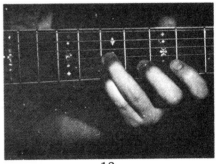
12

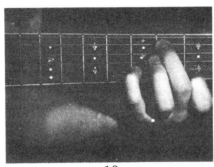
13

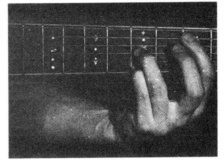
14

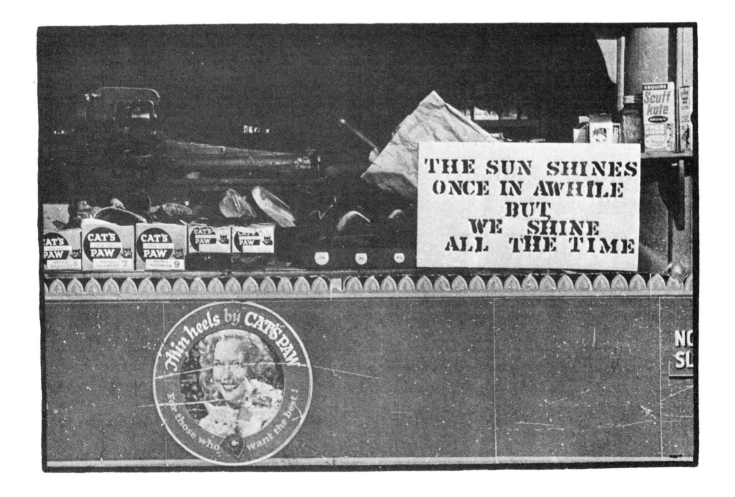

Piano Sounds

This is a very interesting instrumental put together by Marc Silber. It is an imitation of a piano boogie played in the key of D. I have only transcribed one section as this will give you a good idea of what type of sound Marc was looking for. It is an excellent example of a country blues sound put into the city idiom of the 1960's. Perhaps the forerunner of *Piano Sounds* is *Mississippi Blues* by Willie Brown, which is another boogie played on the guitar but with a strong piano flavor. This piece has been translated in my Oak book *The Delta Blues Guitar*.

Piano Sounds begins with a walking bass almost identical to Jelly Roll Morton's *Buddy Bolden Blues*. But once you begin playing the fourth chord, the bass changes to a straight boogie woogie. The end section is most unusual and should offer you a challenge. Marc had a special manner of rolling his bass strings. He would break up a steady alternating rhythm by adding triplets. This gives a very special effect to the piece. He also adapted certain Fats Domino phrases to play as bass figures in the other sections of this instrumental.

I have recorded a similar tune called *Yazoo Basin Boogie* on the Transatlantic Record with that same title. You might find this very helpful.

The guitar is tuned to a drop D tuning: D A D G B E.

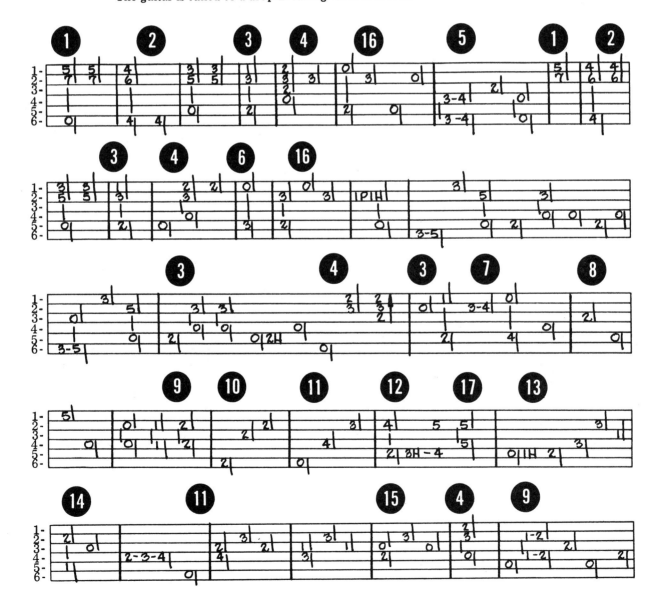

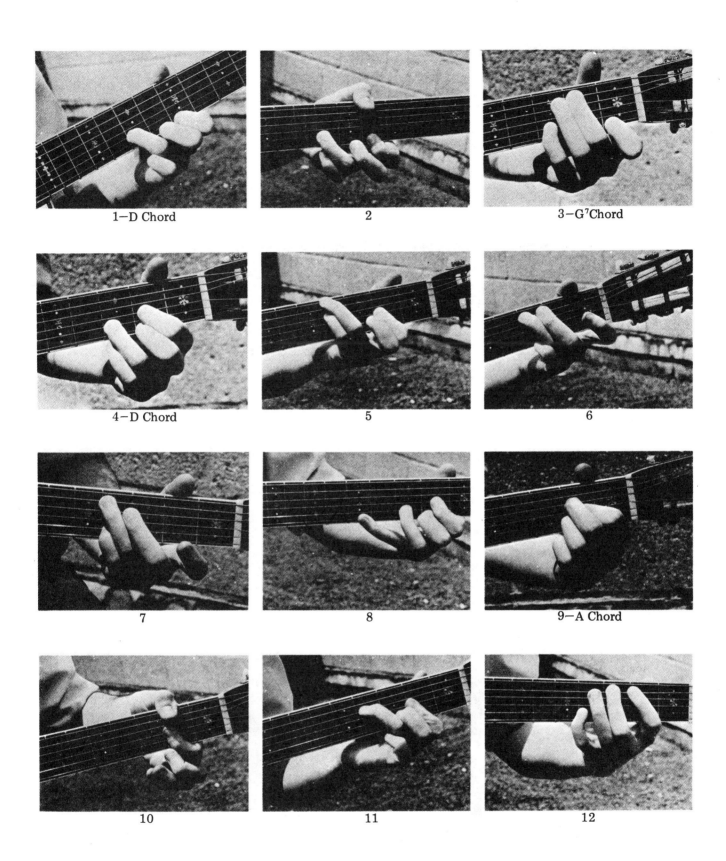

1–D Chord

2

3–G⁷Chord

4–D Chord

5

6

7

8

9–A Chord

10

11

12

Piano Sounds

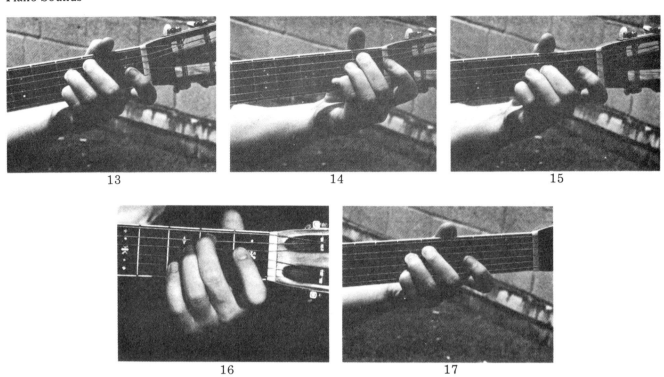

13   14   15

16   17

Rock Boogie In G Ackward

When I first became involved in the guitar techniques of the blues and counterpoint melodies, I found that there were few pieces that combined both. As a result I composed several tunes to help me practice this approach. *Rock Boogie in G Ackward* is one such tune.

The original idea for this piece was taken from the playing of Bruce Langhorne. I had watched him play a piece on the guitar that had the bass playing a boogie figure and above this a melody and improvised statements on the treble strings. What had interested me was that the bass figure never stopped, no matter how difficult the left hand fingering might be. I thought that this was quite a unique style. Instead of the guitar imitating a piano, it was using a boogie theme within the framework of the sounds a guitar could produce. The result is that two very distinct lines are heard.

This piece has no tricky timing. Instead of an alternating bass we have a steady bass line being played on every beat. The rhythm is then divided into a series of "pinch — hit, pinch — hit, pinch — hit".

The guitar is tuned regularly. Once you have mastered this, I suggest you compare the results to the previous selection, *Piano Sounds.* Both tunes are boogies but each achieves a different effect.

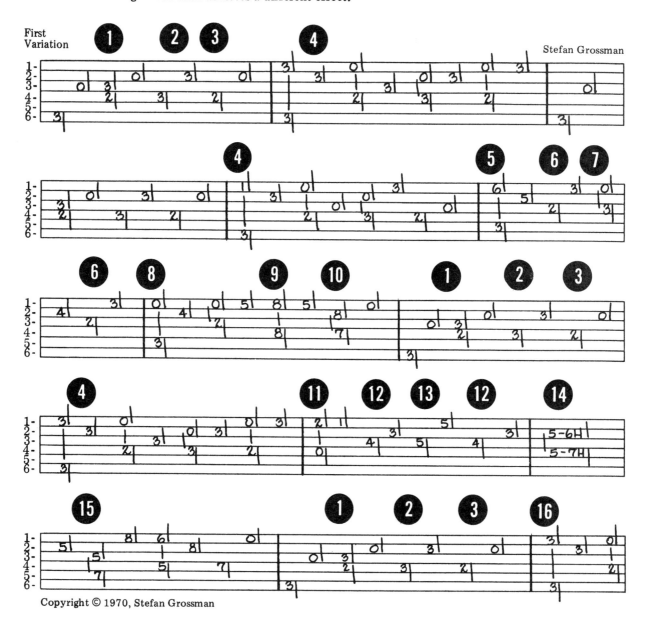

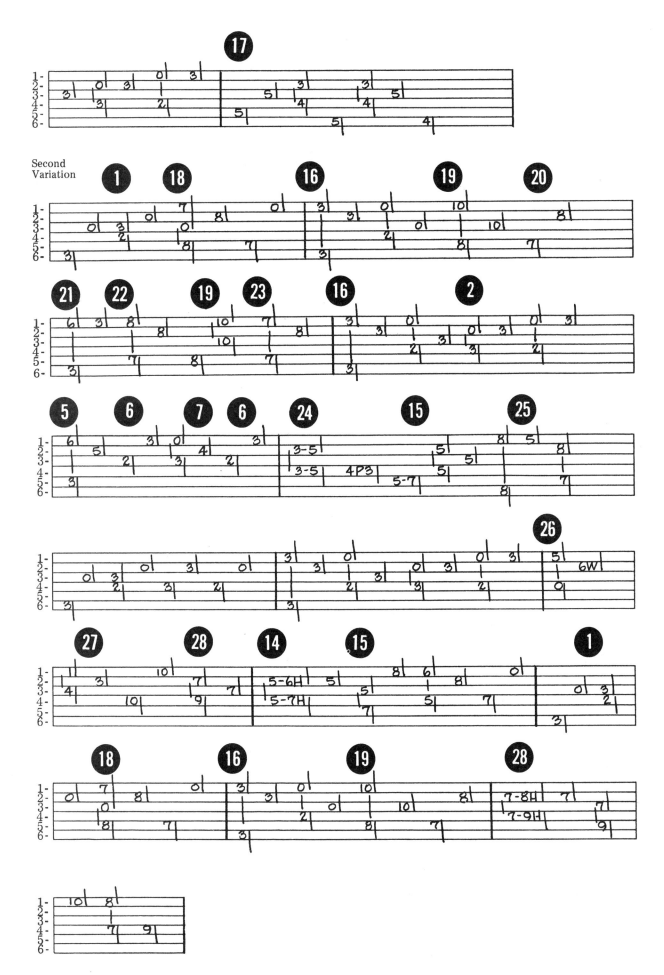

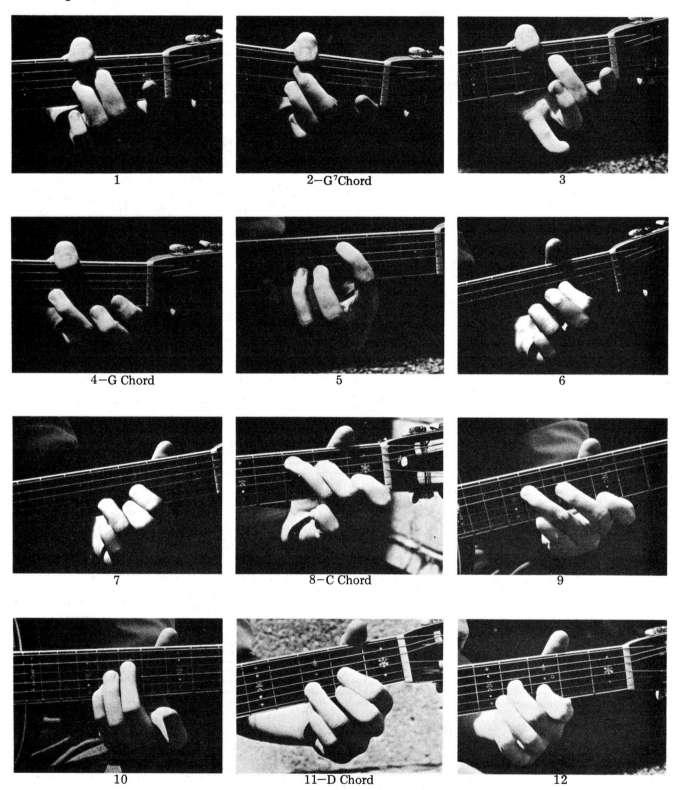

1

2—G⁷Chord

3

4—G Chord

5

6

7

8—C Chord

9

10

11—D Chord

12

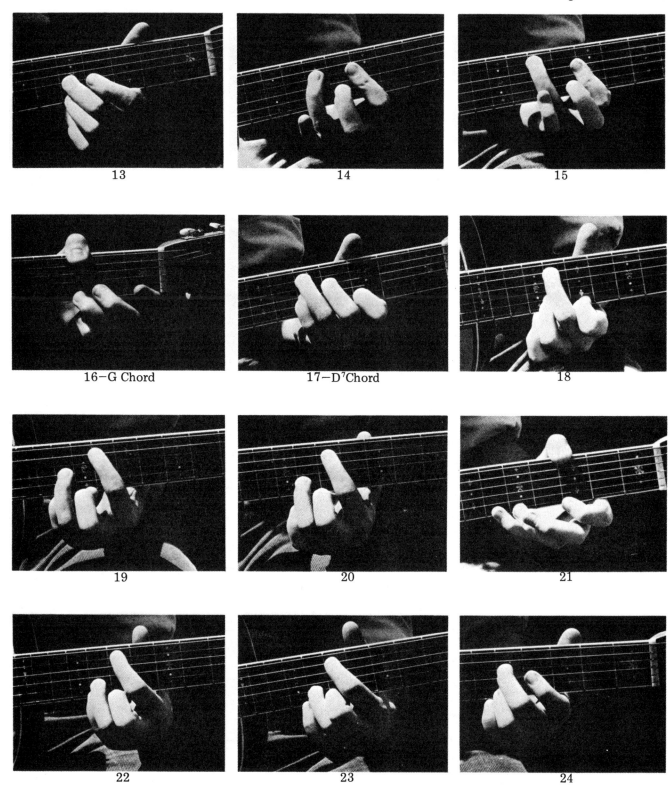

13

14

15

16—G Chord

17—D⁷Chord

18

19

20

21

22

23

24

Rock Boogie In G Ackward

25 26 27

28

Slow Blues In C

The key of C is probably the most popular key for guitar instrumentals and accompaniments. Most of Mississippi John Hurt's, Frank Stoke's, Sam McGee's, Rev. Gary Davis' and Blind Blake's tunes are played in this key. Each uses a different style and as a result produces distinct sounds though they all have their origin in the key of C. I can find no reason for this preference but I suppose it offers a hidden convenience that I have not yet found. It does have a certain color to it and it also seems like the *natural* key for playing music on the guitar.

This selection is simply a *Slow Blues in C.* Unlike other pieces that I have transcribed in C for my *Country Blues Guitar Series* this one has a *walking bass* somewhat in the style of a slow blues on a piano. In fact, the second section (when the guitar modulates to the F chord) is taken from the playing of Jelly Roll Morton. This tune should be a challenge. I suggest once you have mastered it that you add on sections in other styles. You can find some ideas from my book *Ragtime Blues Guitarists* also by Oak. These songs might prove useful:

Black Dog Blues by Blind Blake
Black Horse Blues by Blind Lemon Jefferson
Shuffle Rag by Big Bill Broonzy
You've Got Something There by Blind Boy Fuller

I have recorded this piece with several variations on the album *Yazoo Basin Boogie.*

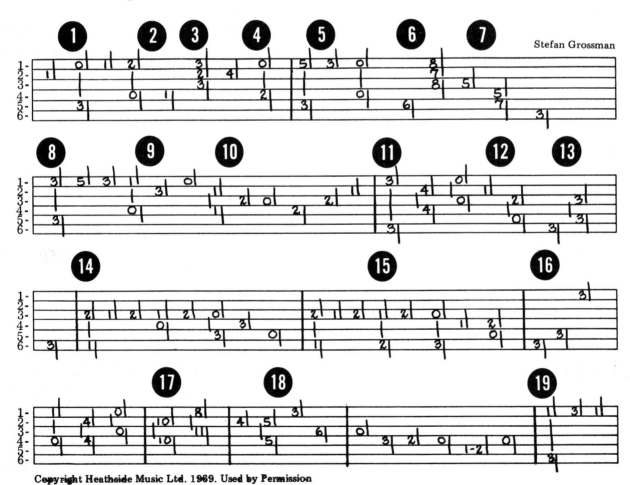

Stefan Grossman

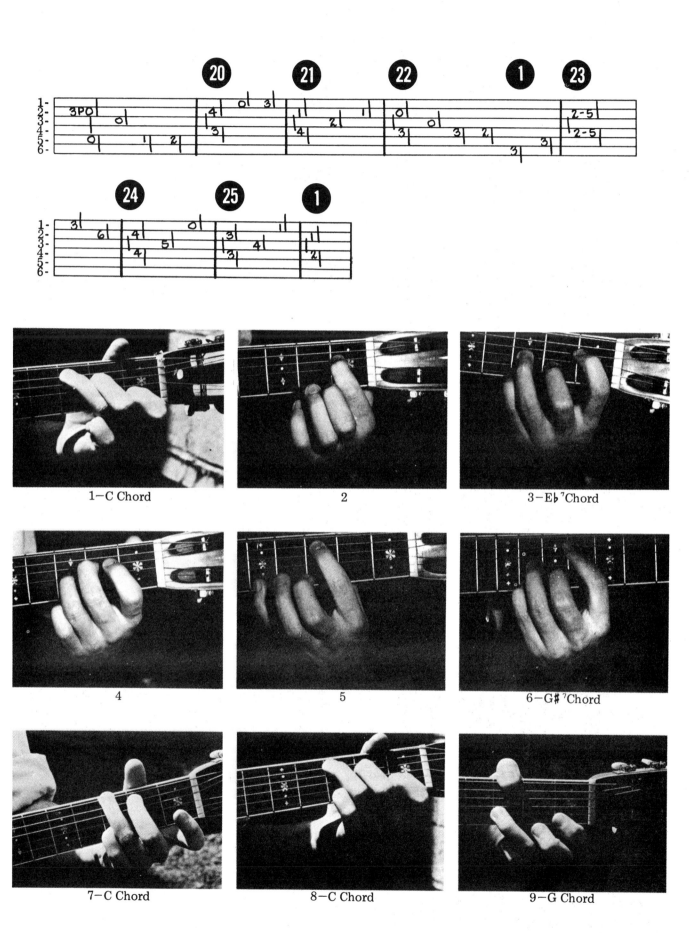

1—C Chord

2

3—E♭⁷ Chord

4

5

6—G♯⁷ Chord

7—C Chord

8—C Chord

9—G Chord

Slow Blues In C

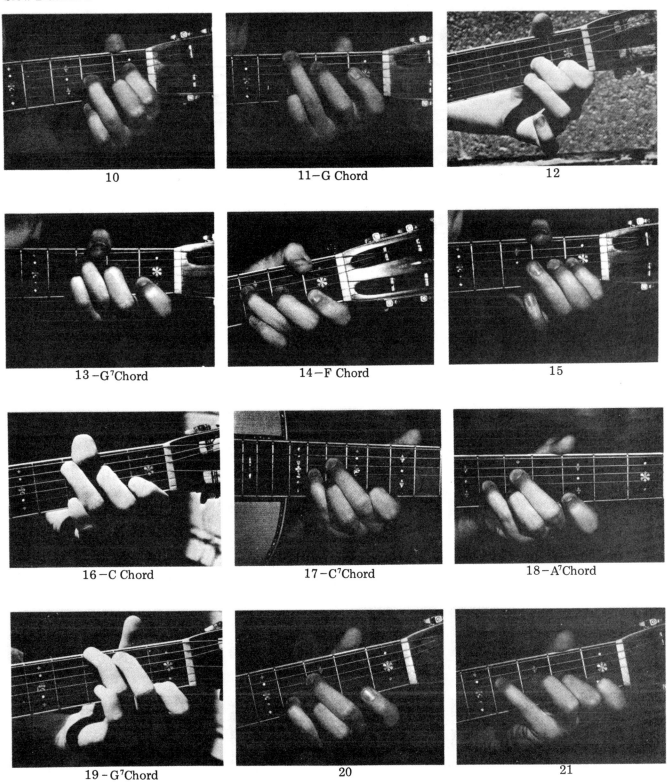

10

11—G Chord

12

13—G⁷Chord

14—F Chord

15

16—C Chord

17—C⁷Chord

18—A⁷Chord

19 – G⁷Chord

20

21

22

23

24

25

Fiddle Tunes

Money's All Gone

This is a fiddle tune transcribed for the guitar. This type of music presents certain challenges and each piece in this section will show a different approach.

Money's All Gone is a very melodic tune put together with an alternating bass style. It is played in the key of A and the guitar is in a regular tuning. The bass alternates between the sixth and fifth strings and this produces a drone-like effect. You must be mindful to put an accent on the second and fourth beats of each measure; it will give this tune a special feeling. There is a counterpoint end tag in the first section which puts a nice variation to the constantly alternating bass.

The guitar will almost sound like the Northumberland pipes if you stress the even beats. As on the pipes, a drone is first established and then the melody flows over it.

This piece was arranged by Dave Laibman from a recording by the New Lost City Ramblers. This is the first of Dave's pieces that we will print here but many others will follow. He had a unique talent for making the guitar sound like any instrument he desired. As you will see in the Ragtime Section, he was also able to develop counterpoint lines that enhance the piece.

I have recorded this arrangement on my Fontana disc: *Aunt Molly's Murray Farm* (Kicking Mule Records, Sonet Records).

Money's All Gone

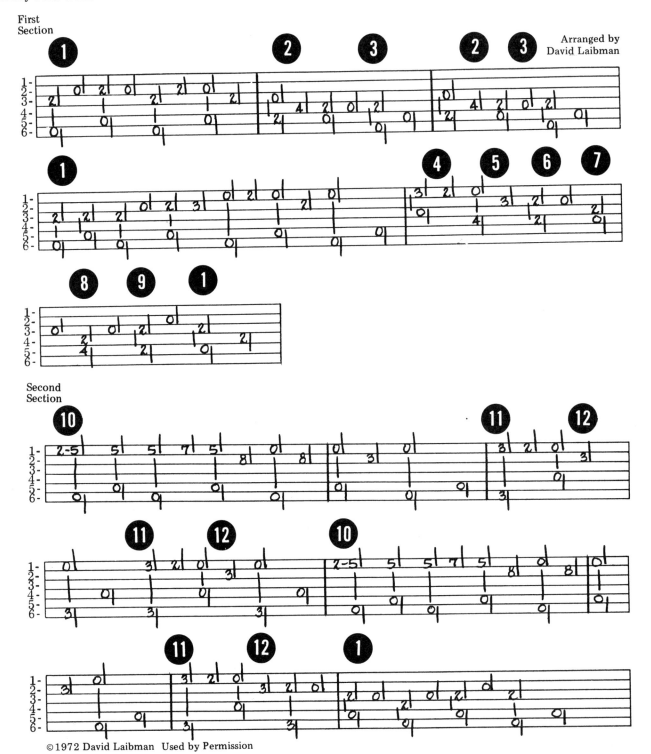

28

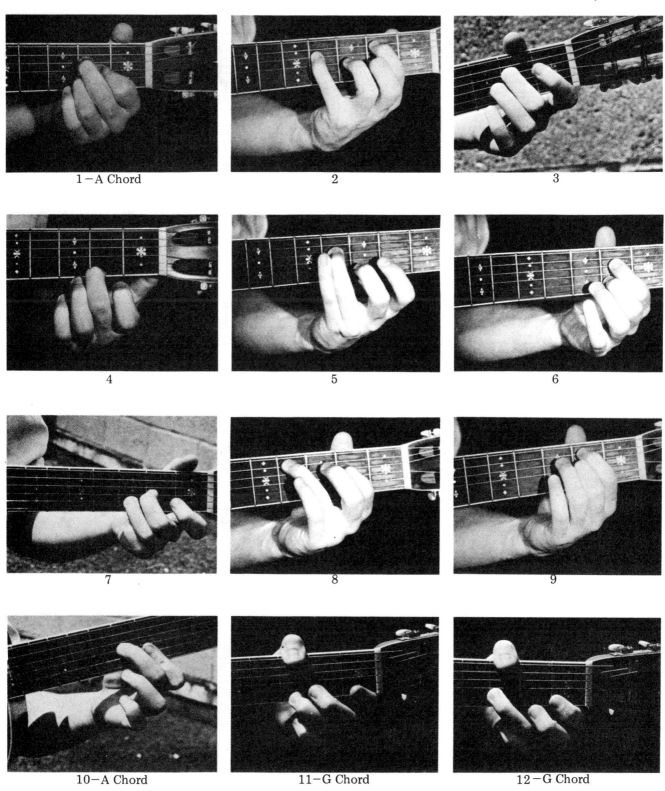

1 — A Chord   2   3

4   5   6

7   8   9

10 — A Chord   11 — G Chord   12 — G Chord

Money's All Gone

Colored Aristocracy

This is another arrangement by Dave Laibman but this time in a more Nashville style reminiscent of Chet Atkins or Merle Travis. The guitar is in regular tuning and this piece is played in the key of A. Please take note that *Money's All Gone* was also played in this key, yet the end result was quite different in sound.

This is a fast-tempo fiddle tune and the guitar uses an alternating bass technique coupled with the use of some ingenious chord structures. These unorthodox chord fingerings enable us to maintain our bass and still play all the necessary melody notes. This is another characteristic of Dave's playing. When he needs a special chord he is not afraid of inventing it. If you strummed the guitar while playing one of these *home-made* chords the result would be quite discordant. But since we are not strumming this problem does not come up. You simply must be careful to play all the correct strings at the proper time. If you do not, this happy American dance tune might end up sounding like an Eastern European dirge.

If you are interested in this type of sound I suggest you listen to any recording by Doc Watson, Chet Atkins or Merle Travis. I myself have recorded *Colored Aristocracy* on my Transatlantic disc *Yazoo Basin Boogie*.

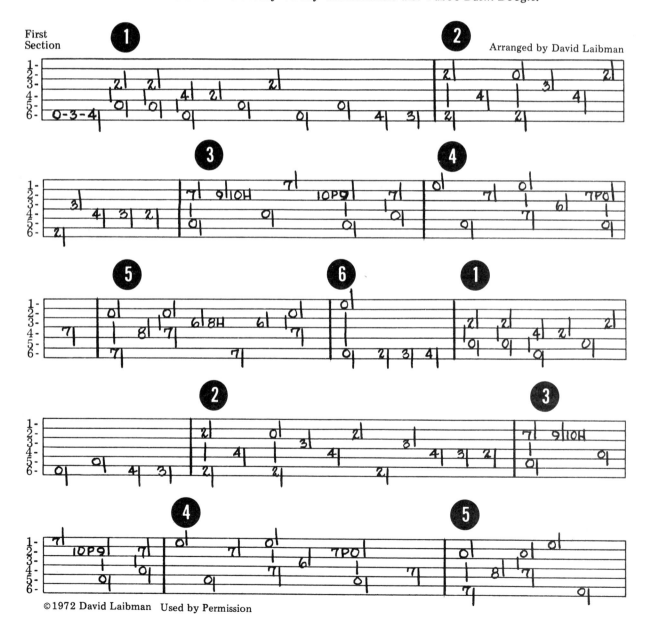

Colored Aristocracy

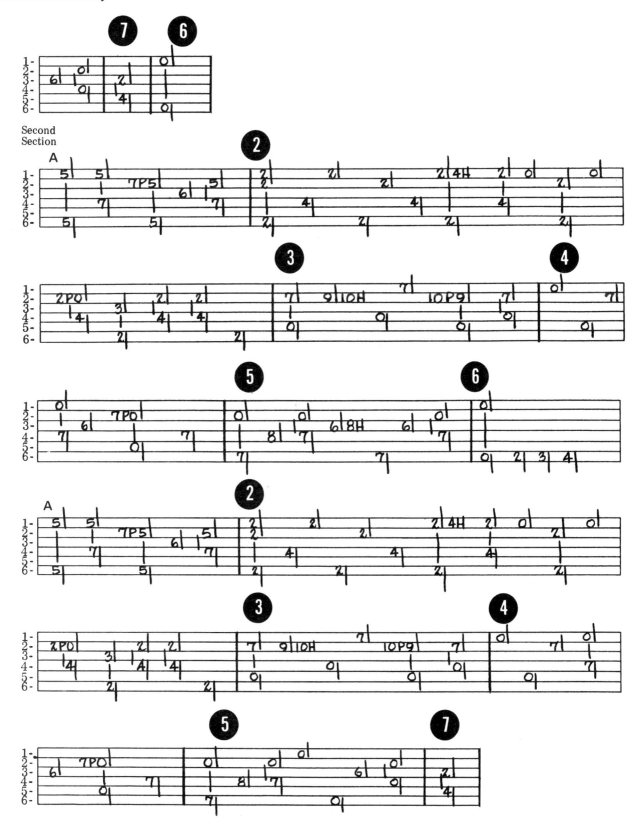

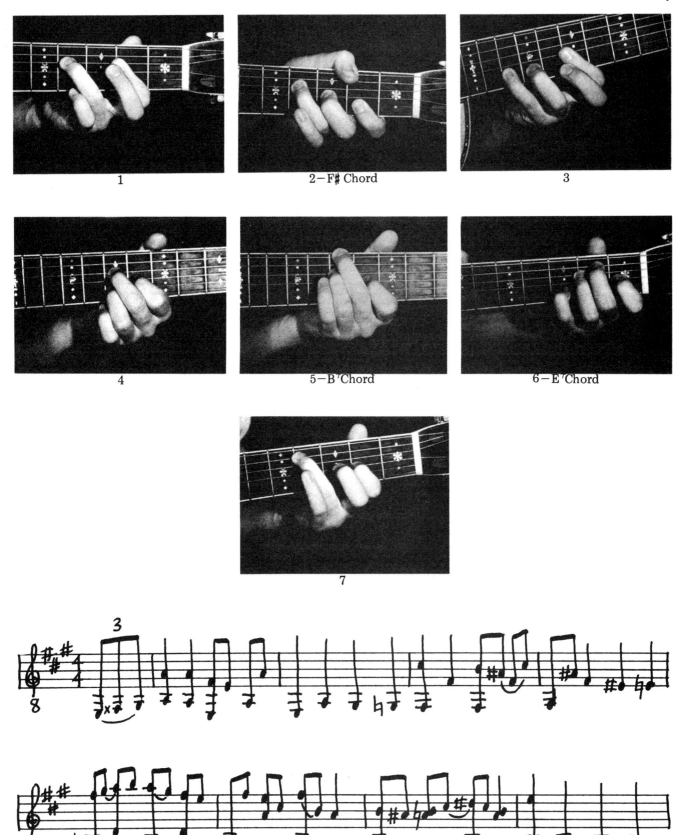

1

2—F♯ Chord

3

4

5—B⁷ Chord

6—E⁷ Chord

7

Colored Aristocracy

Pigtown Fling

I first heard *Pigtown Fling* played on the mandolin by George Roberts in Ann Arbor, Michigan. I very much liked the unusual quality of the tune. It is divided into two sections both of which complement each other. The second part especially intrigued me with its use of minor chords. I tried to think of an interesting arrangement and came up with the idea of putting the melody on the treble strings of the guitar and then superimposing a classical type of counterpoint. In order to do this I devised an open tuning where the guitar is tuned: D G D G B E. This is almost identical to an open G tuning only the high E string is not lowered.

This tuning permits us to keep a steady line going while we play the tune on the high strings. There is nothing complicated to the rhythm but I suggest you follow the chord photographs carefully to play all the fingerings properly.

This piece has been recorded on my Transatlantic disc *Yazoo Basin Boogie*.

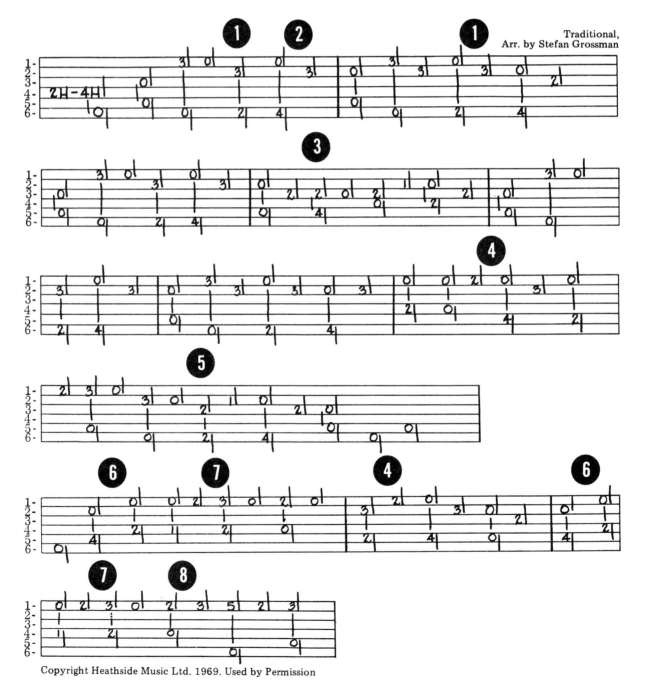

Traditional,
Arr. by Stefan Grossman

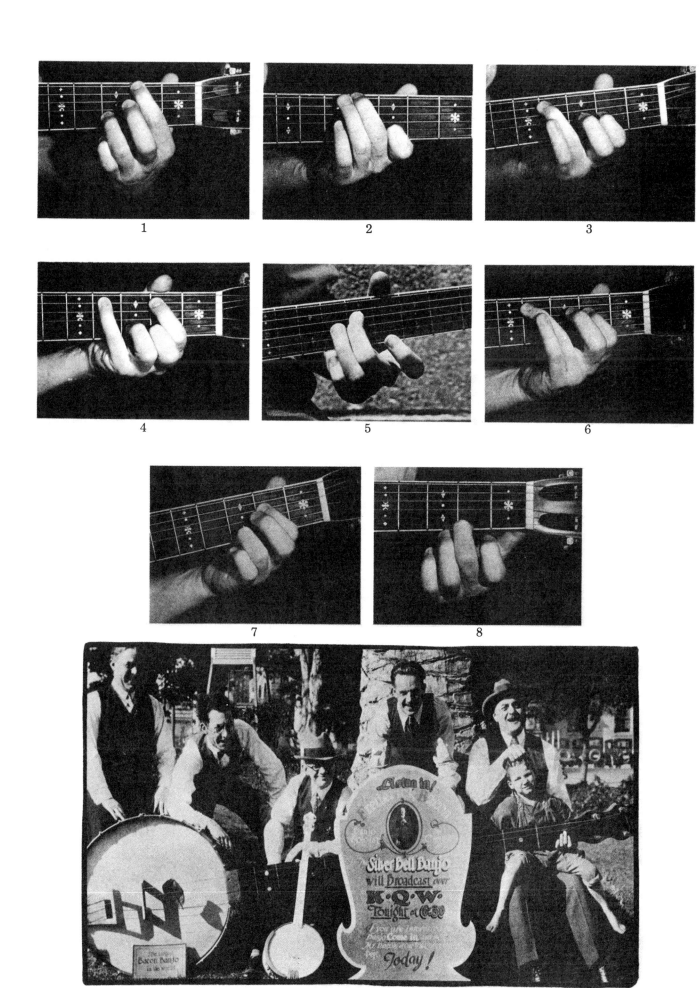

1

2

3

4

5

6

7

8

Pigtown Fling

Miss McLeod's Reel

This piece is very similar in approach to *Rock Boogie in G Ackward*. I first became involved in counterpoint techniques when I had to invent some songs to act as exercises. I took the melody from *Miss McLeod's Reel* and then placed over it a simple boogie woogie bass line. Luckily the bass figure was harmonically right for the melody. At first I wrote each section in tablature and then tried to play them part by part. It took me many months to master the technique of combining two lines together on the guitar.

The guitar is tuned as in *Pigtown Fling*: D G D G B E, but in this song the sixth string is never played. You can hear a tape of this by writing to:

Black Patty Tape Service
c/o Grossman
32 Gramercy Park South
New York City, 10003 New York

It would be a good exercise for you to try re-arranging this tune in the style of *Colored Aristocracy*. Try to use the key of A as it might prove easier.

Traditional, Arr.
by Stefan Grossman

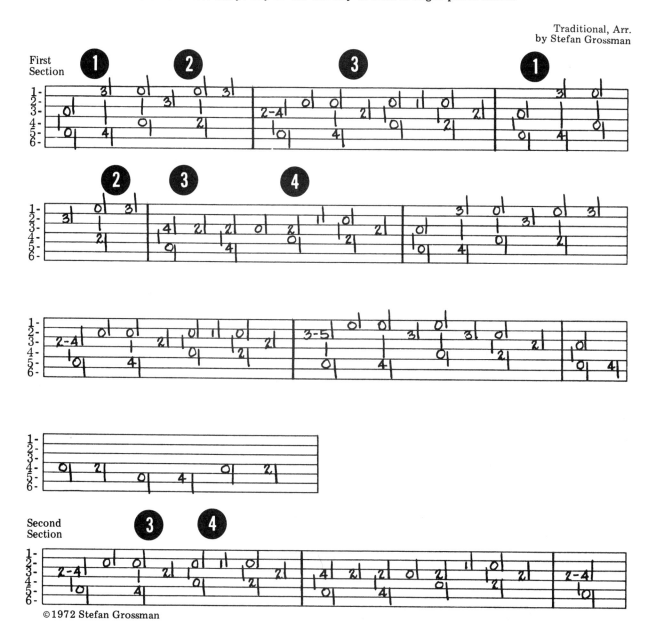

Miss McLeod's Reel

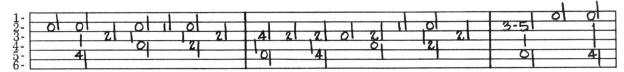

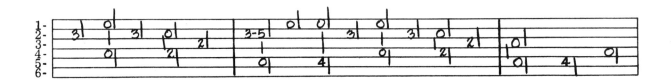

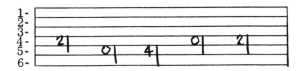

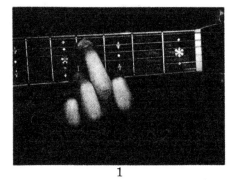

1

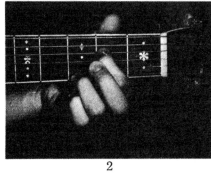

2

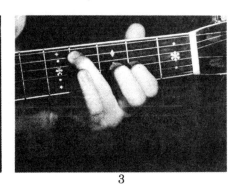

3

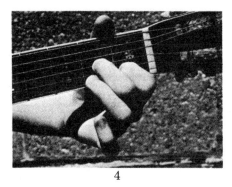

4

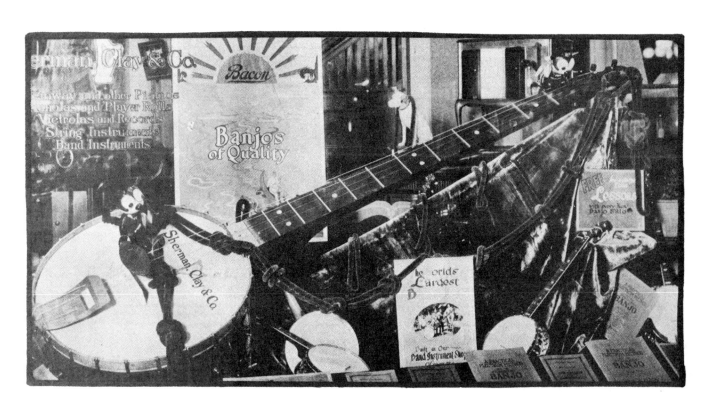

Last Of Callahan/Dervish Boogie

This is a beautiful arrangement of the old fiddle tune *Last of Callahan/Dervish Boogie*. It was developed by Dave Laibman. The bass plays a boogie pattern somewhat similar to our arrangement of *Miss McLeod's Reel* but in this case the bass line merges with the treble melodic line to produce a more unified sound. It is a very tricky piece of guitar playing. The guitar is tuned to a dropped D tuning: D A D G B E and the whole piece is basically played around a simple D chord. Your index and last fingers do most of the work, relying on pull-offs and hammer-ons.

I have recorded this on my Transatlantic record *Yazoo Basin Boogie*. You can hear the original on the Library of Congress recording entitled: *Anglo-American Shanties, Lyric Songs, Dance Tunes and Spirituals AAFS L2.* You can obtain a catalogue of all their available records by writing:
Recording Laboratory
Library of Congress
Washington 25, D.C.

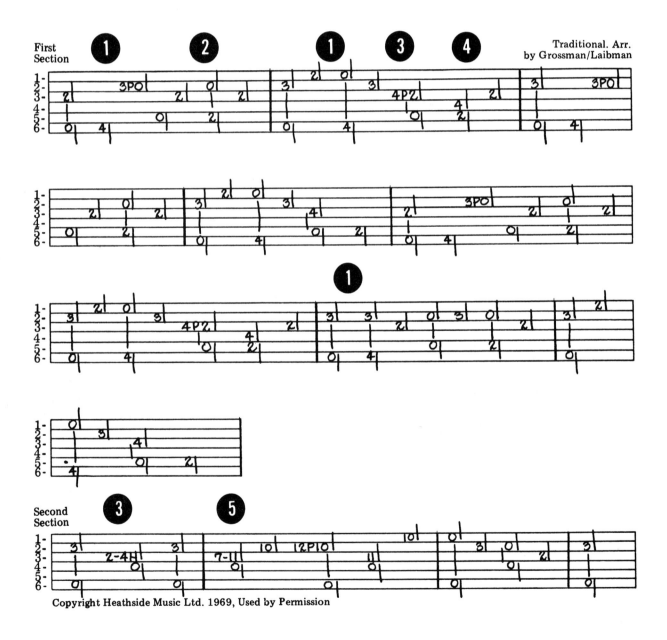

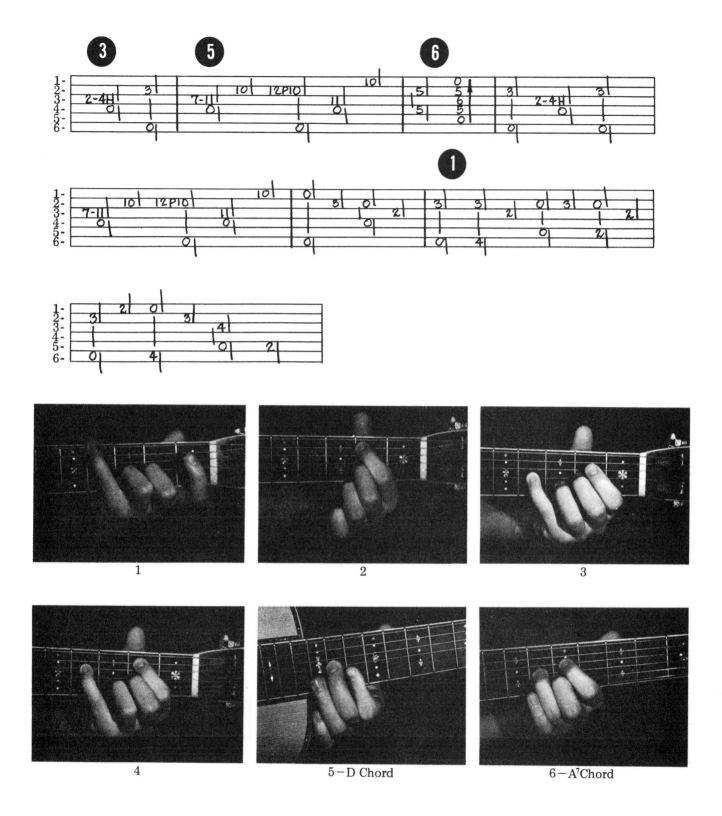

1

2

3

4

5 — D Chord

6 — A⁷Chord

Last of Callahan/Dervish Boogie

Cakewalks And Classic Piano Rags

Dallas Rag

We begin our section on cakewalks and piano classic rags by taking an old string-band tune called *Dallas Rag*. This is perhaps the most popular rag to be played on the guitar. You can hear an interesting old-timey version on a recording by the New Lost City Ramblers. Dave Laibman took this performance and transcribed it for the guitar. Essentially, the mandolin part is played on the treble strings, while the guitar part is played on the bass strings. Putting them both together gives us a very happy sound which is difficult to produce.

There are many chords in this arrangement that are unorthodox and will take some finger-stretching to get used to. I usually put a capo on the second fret of my guitar to make playing this tune easier. There are also several difficult single-string runs. When you play these I suggest that you carefully read the tablature for which right-hand fingers you should be using.

I have not thought it necessary to properly label all the chords used. As in *Colored Aristocracy* (which was also arranged by Dave Laibman), there are chords that cannot be strummed. They have been devised to make the playing easier but do not necessarily make the right hand fingering simpler. You must be very careful to play all the proper strings at the right time.

This song combines three techniques. The main theme is played with an alternating bass style while a counterpoint approach is used for many end tags. A single-string style is used for end tags and breaks.

What makes this such a successful arrangement is the juxtaposition of all three styles. The guitar is tuned in a regular tuning. I have recorded this version of *Dallas Rag* on my disc *Yazoo Basin Boogie*.

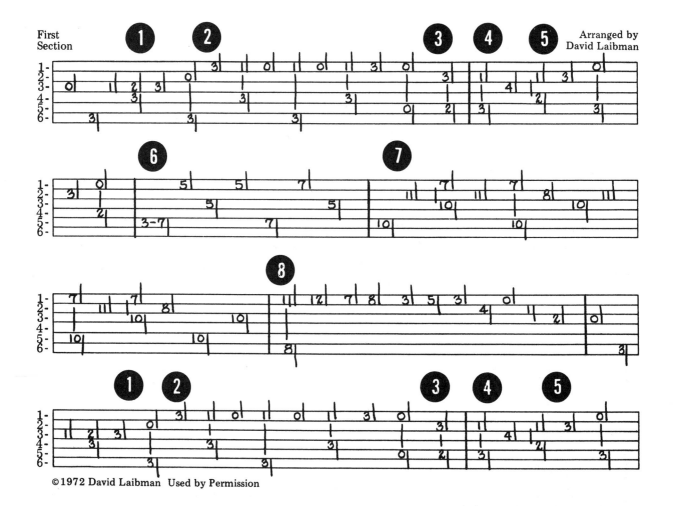

Arranged by
David Laibman

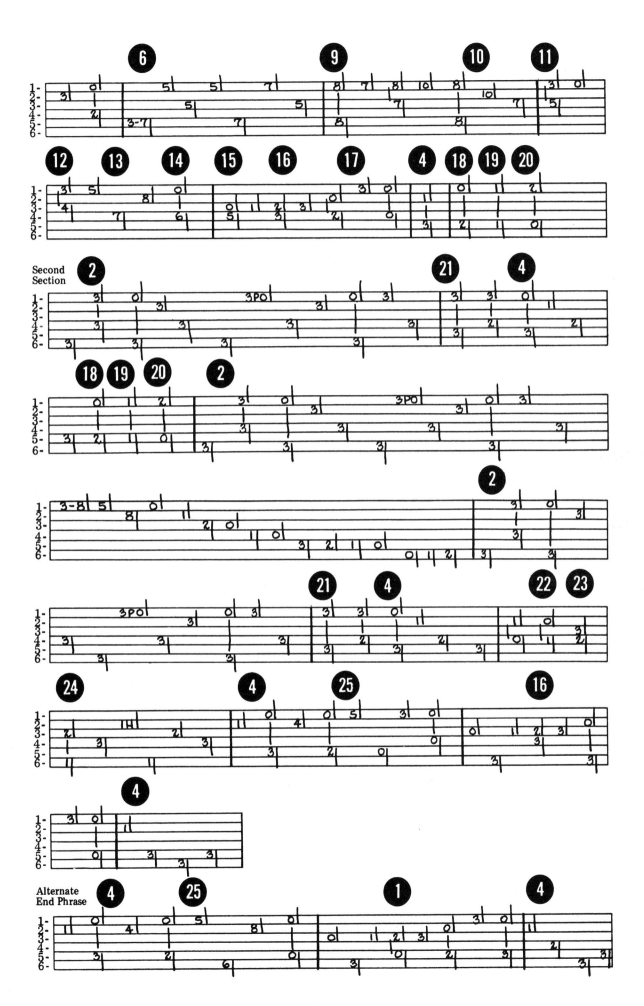

Dallas Rag

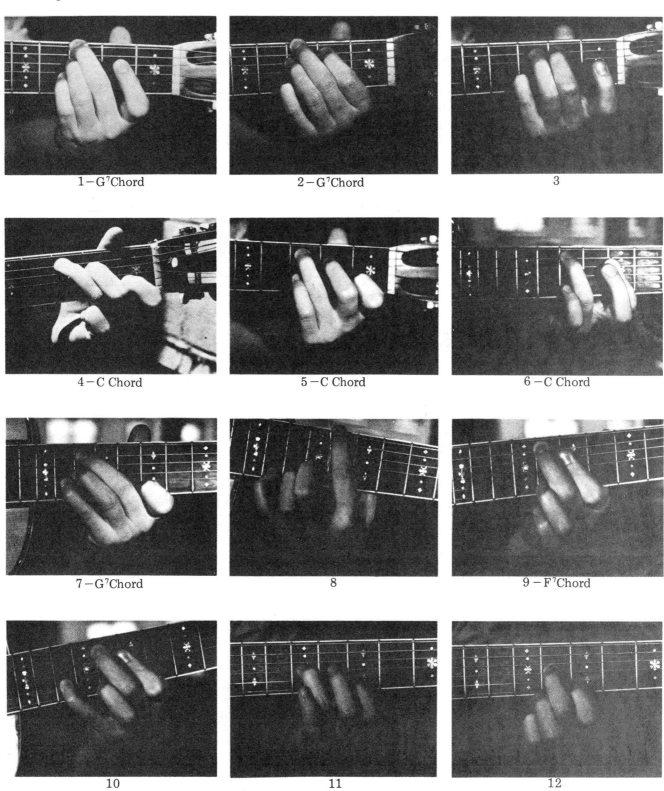

1 — G⁷Chord   2 — G⁷Chord   3

4 — C Chord   5 — C Chord   6 — C Chord

7 — G⁷Chord   8   9 — F⁷Chord

10   11   12

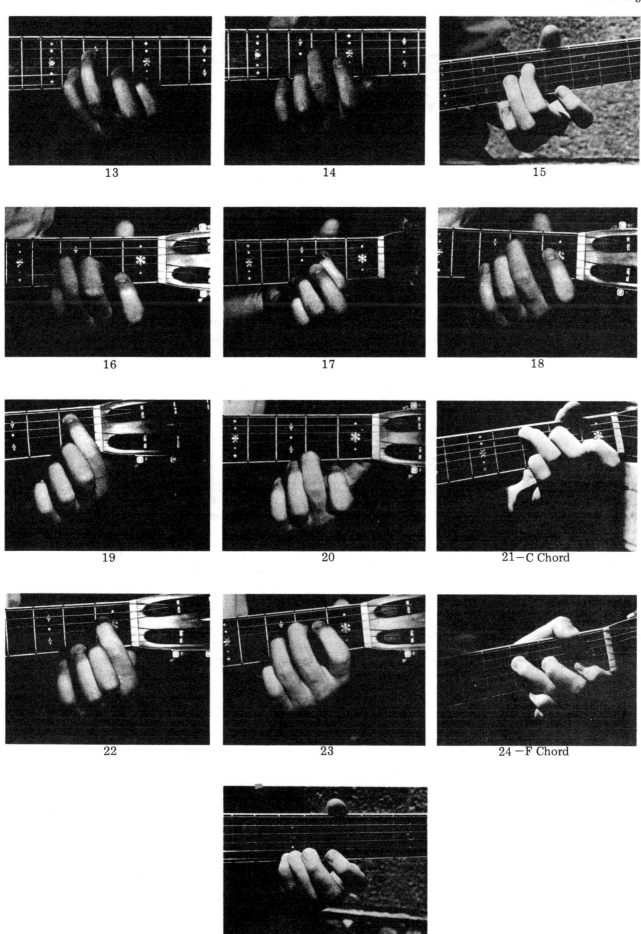

13

14

15

16

17

18

19

20

21—C Chord

22

23

24 —F Chord

25

Dallas Rag

Dallas Rag

Original Rags

Original Rags was written at the turn of the century by Scott Joplin. It is an example of what has been called a classic piano rag. This tune was arranged for the guitar by Eric Kaz, who is a very talented guitar, harmonica and piano player. Eric took the first two sections of this four part rag and first learnt them on the piano. He then transcribed the notes to play them on the guitar. It is quite simple and played in a regular tuning. It is played in the key of C.

The tablature shows a variation for an end tag that might prove interesting. Also take note that the first section should be played twice, then the second and finally back to the first. You might find a challenge in trying to arrange the last two sections of this rag. You can find many old piano roll re-issue records of this piece.

You can get a tape of this tune from Black Patty Tape Service.

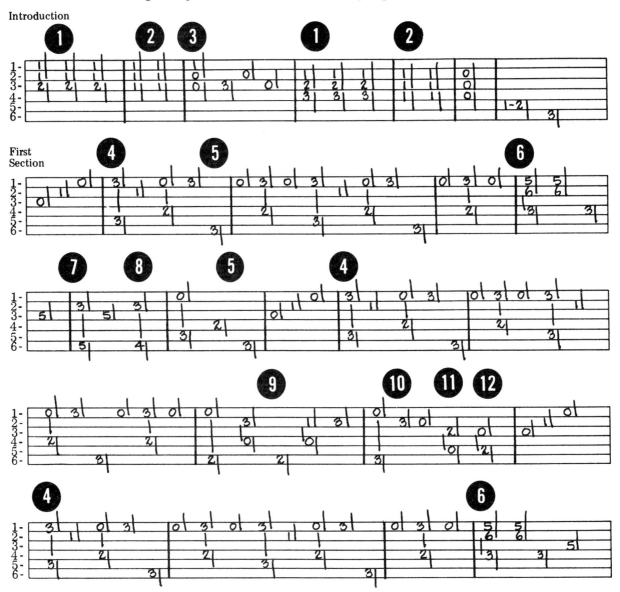

Variation to A and D7:
Second Time Through

Second
Section

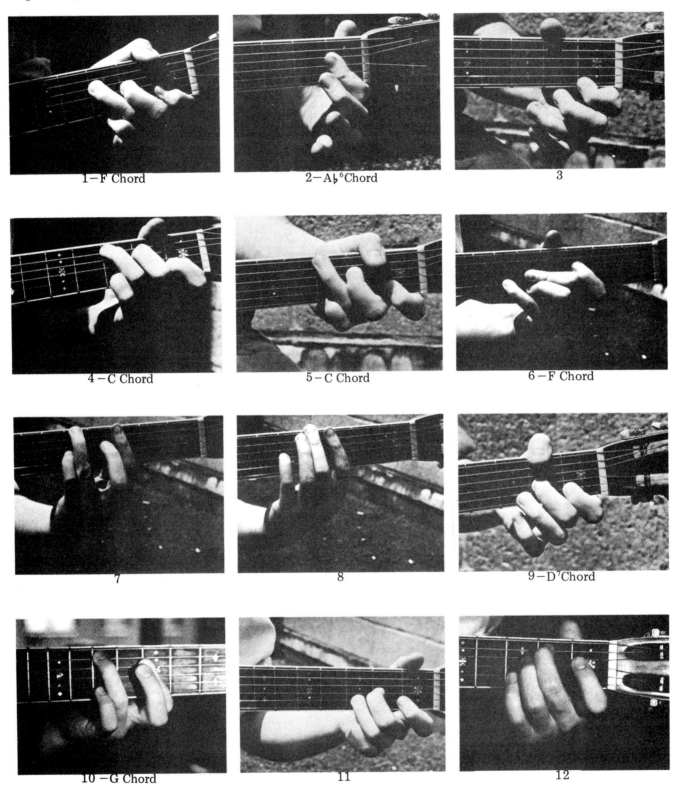

1—F Chord

2—Ab⁶ Chord

3

4 — C Chord

5 — C Chord

6 — F Chord

7

8

9—D⁷ Chord

10 — G Chord

11

12

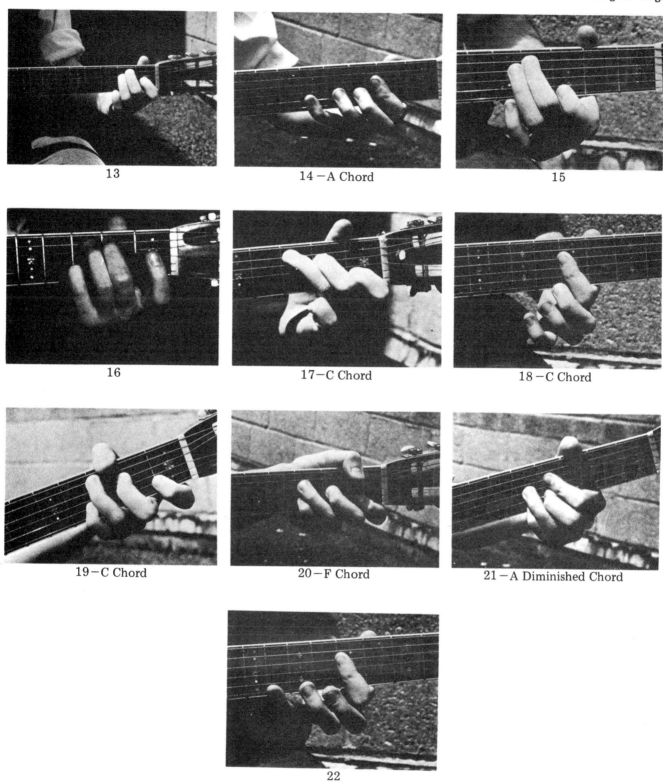

13

14 — A Chord

15

16

17 — C Chord

18 — C Chord

19 — C Chord

20 — F Chord

21 — A Diminished Chord

22

Original Rags

Georgia Camp Meeting

During the Gay Nineties one of the most popular cakewalks was *Georgia Camp Meeting*. You have probably heard it played by brass marching bands during a local football match. Our arrangement was put together by a fine young guitarist named Ric Schoenberg. He has been able to capture the feeling of this cakewalk as if it was being played on an old honky-tonk type piano. He does this by playing it in a regular tuning in the key of A and combining an alternating bass with counter-point lines. This is a very flowing piece and should give you a lot of fun.

This version has three sections transcribed. I have heard one version which played four parts and you can hear this on *The Riverside History of Classic Jazz* (Riverside 12-112, Jazz Archive Series). This is an excellent record which has half a dozen old piano rolls which are all good material to be adapted for the guitar. I have also heard a string band arrangement on the Piedmont disc *Ragtime—A Recorded Documentary*. Both of these records present different approaches to *Georgia Camp Meeting*.

You might find some similarities with this arrangement in *Colored Aristocracy*. Both are played in the key of A and both use a steady bass rhythm.

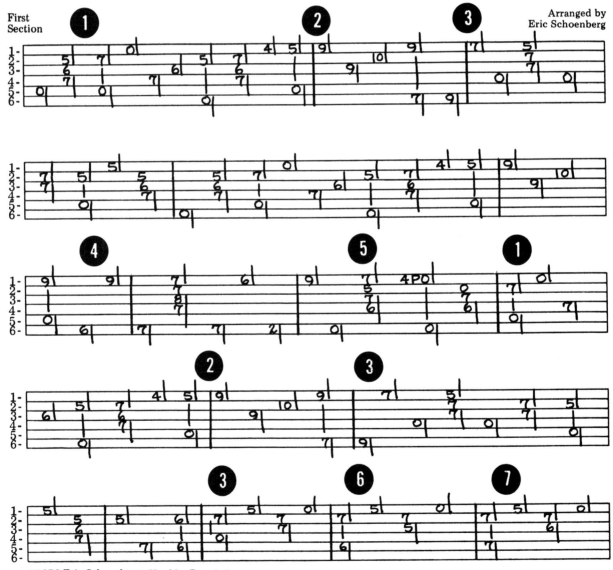

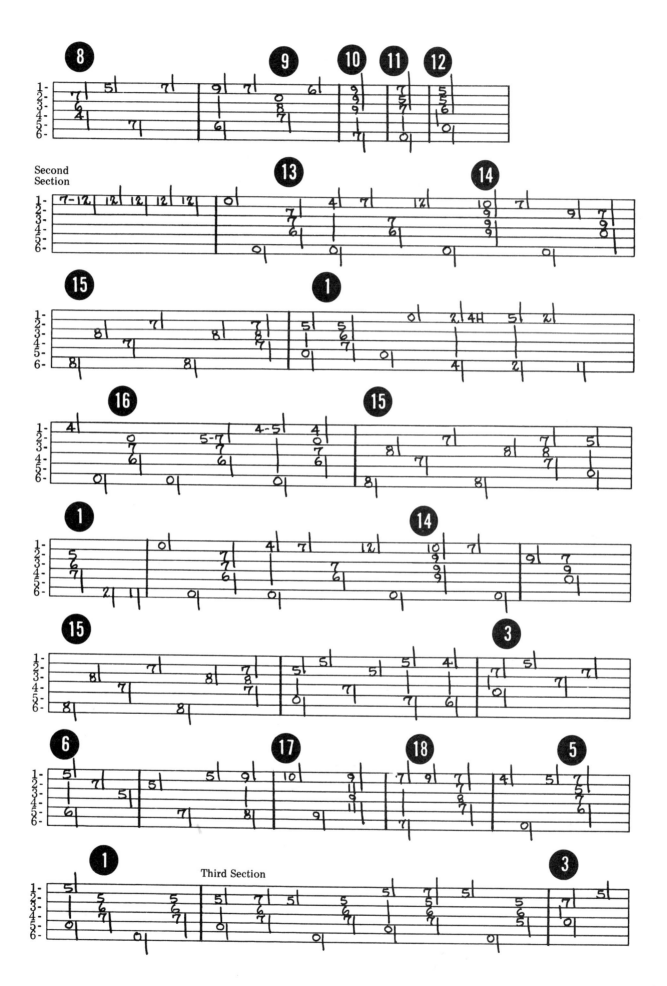

Georgia Camp Meeting

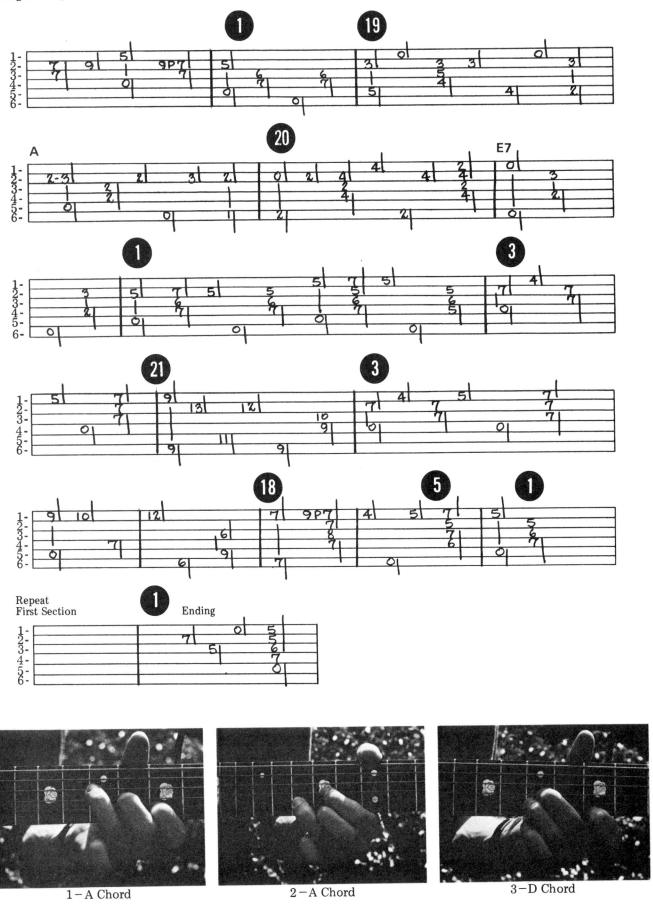

1 – A Chord

2 – A Chord

3 – D Chord

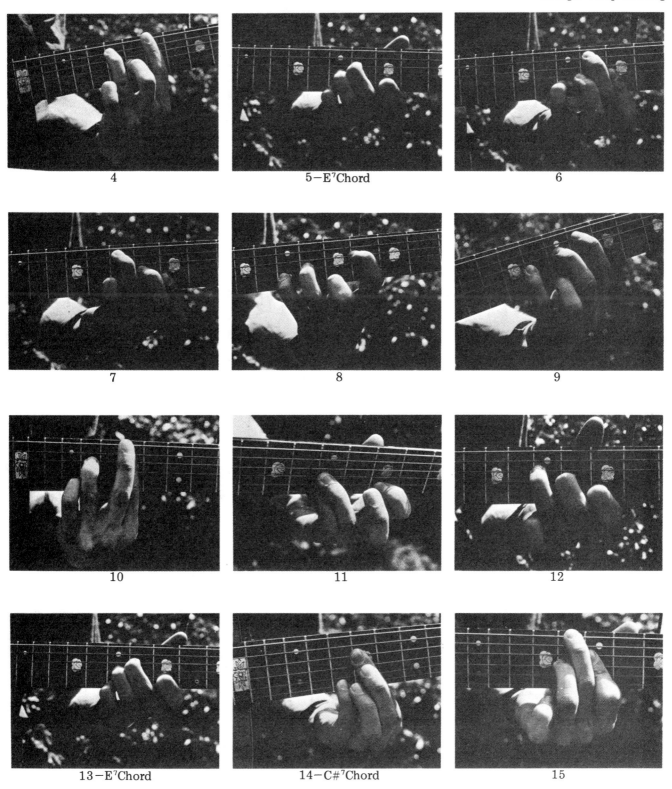

4

5—E⁷Chord

6

7

8

9

10

11

12

13—E⁷Chord

14—C#⁷Chord

15

Georgia Camp Meeting

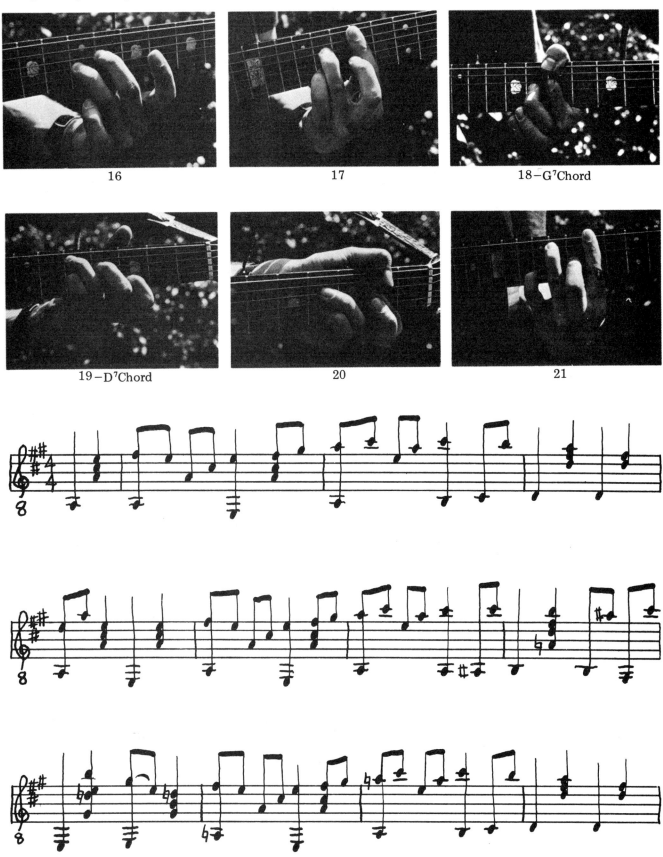

16

17

18 – G⁷Chord

19 – D⁷Chord

20

21

Georgia Camp Meeting

Hilarity Rag

This is another golden oldie. Dave Laibman arranged this for the guitar and you will find it comparatively simple except for the last section. The guitar is in an almost open G tuning: D G D G B E and again I suggest you use a capo on the second fret to make fingering the chords easier. It should be played rapidly with a strongly accented bass.

You can get a recording of this tune by writing to the Black Patty Tape Service.

Arranged by
David Laibman

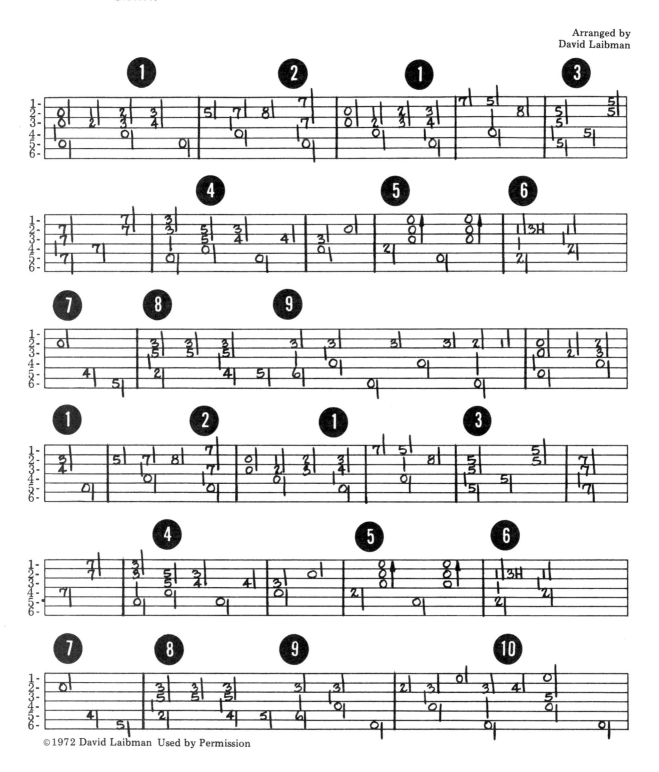

Hilarity Rag

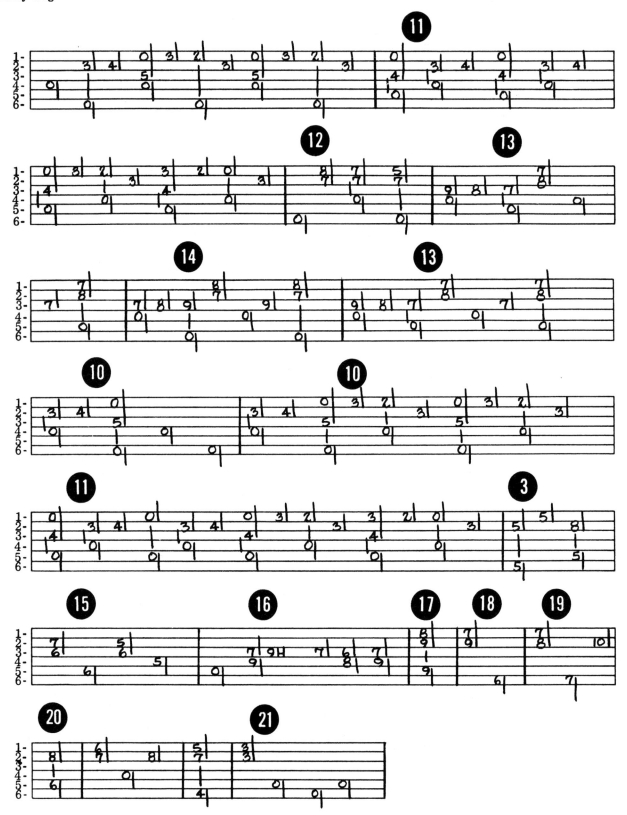

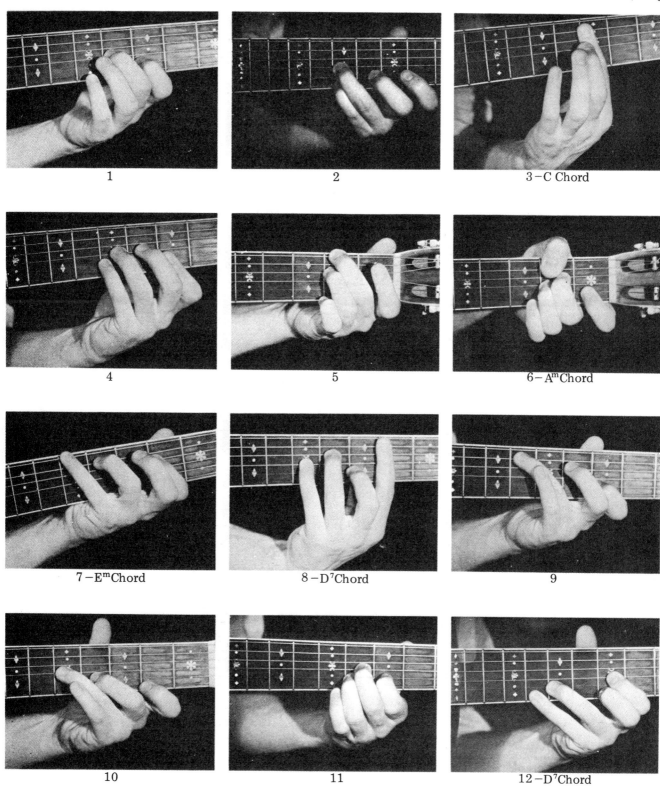

1

2

3 – C Chord

4

5

6 – A^m Chord

7 – E^m Chord

8 – D^7 Chord

9

10

11

12 – D^7 Chord

Hilarity Rag

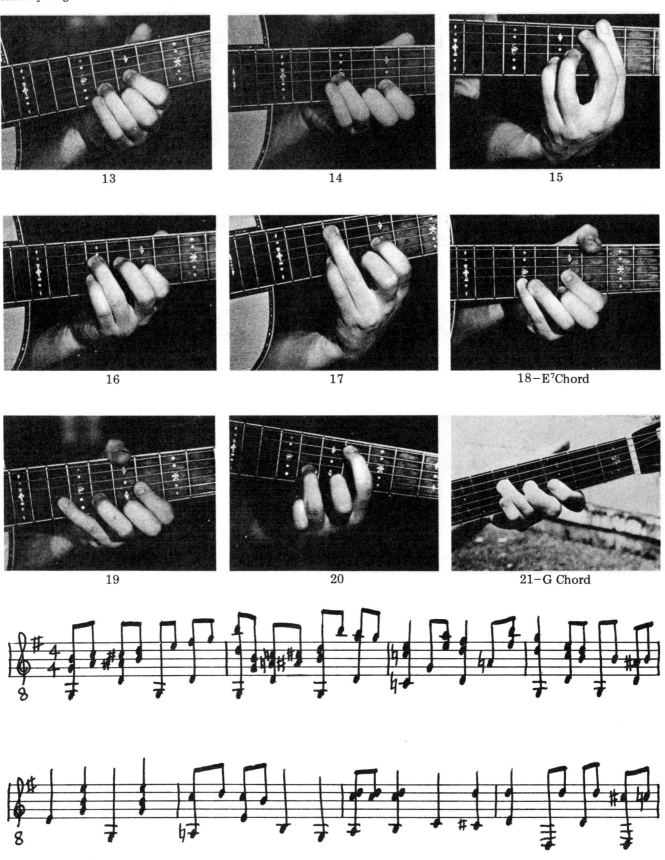

13

14

15

16

17

18—E⁷Chord

19

20

21—G Chord

Maple Leaf Rag

This is an adaptation of the famous Scott Joplin rag. This arrangement only has two sections while the original is composed of four. The second part that we have transcribed is very unlike the original and is a case in point of the *folk-process* where an old piece of music has been used but then changed to fit the liking of the player.

The guitar is tuned to a dropped D tuning: D A D G B E. This is another piece in which you will find it helpful to use a capo on the fourth fret. The first part was arranged by Dave Laibman and follows the original. The second part I arranged and is a variation.

I have recorded this on my Transatlantic disc *Yazoo Basin Boogie*.

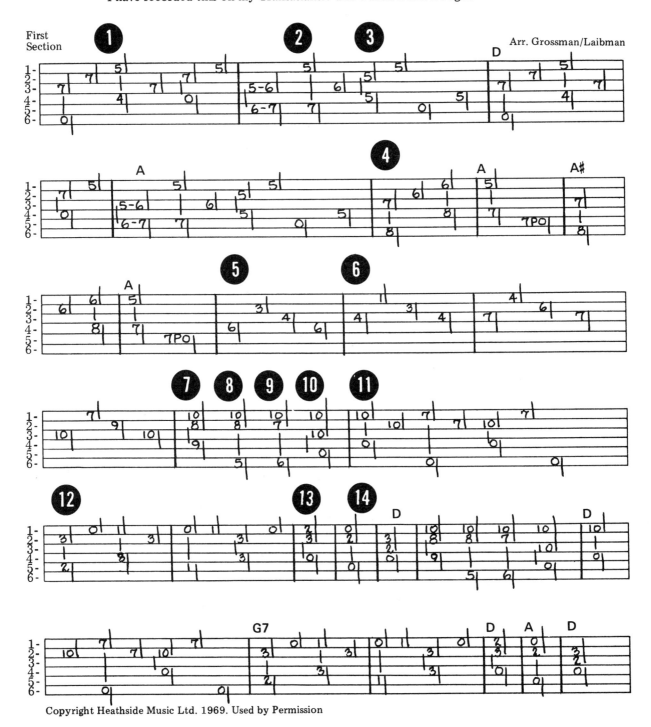

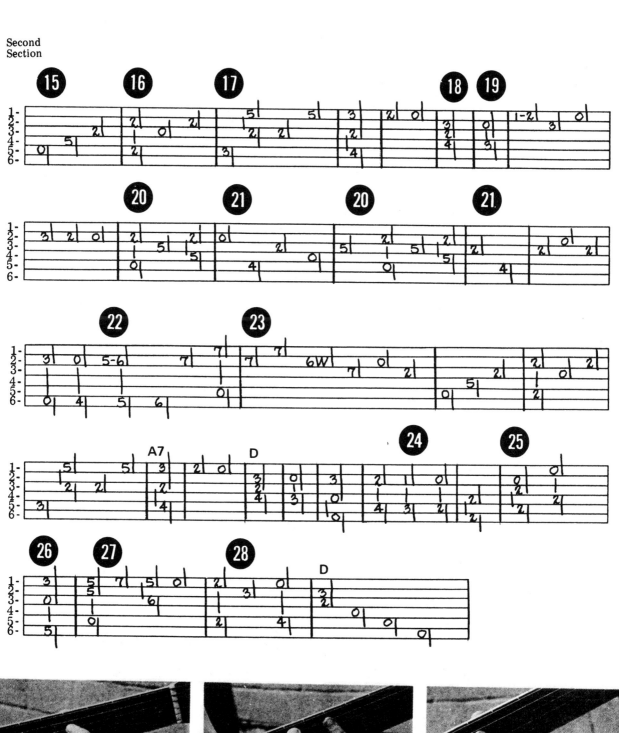

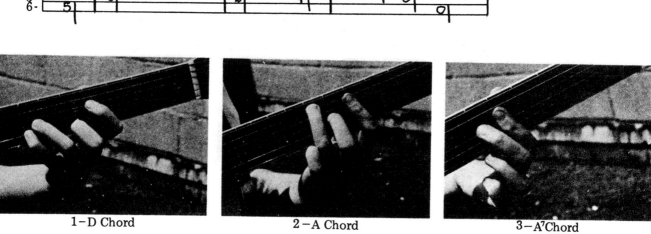

1—D Chord

2—A Chord

3—A⁷Chord

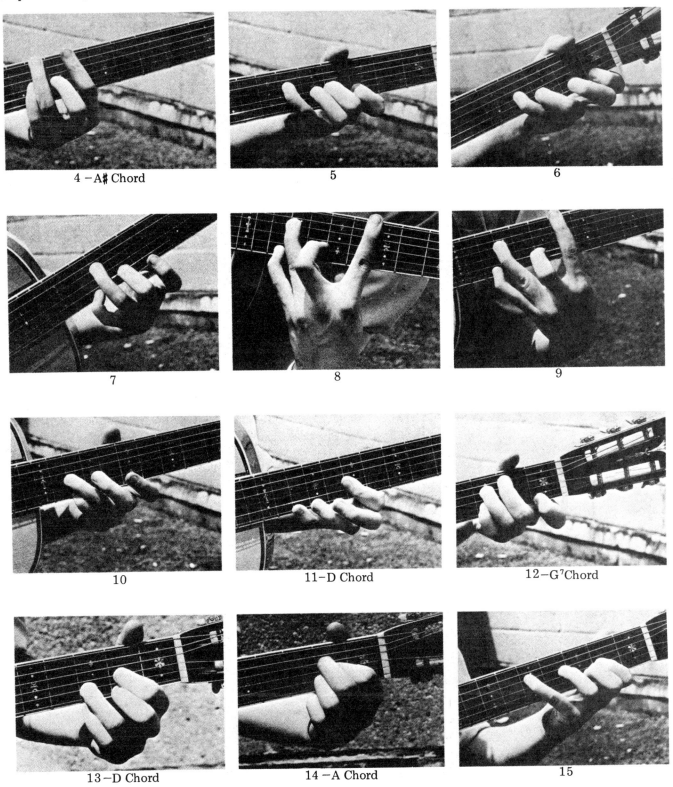

4 – A♯ Chord

5

6

7

8

9

10

11 – D Chord

12 – G⁷ Chord

13 – D Chord

14 – A Chord

15

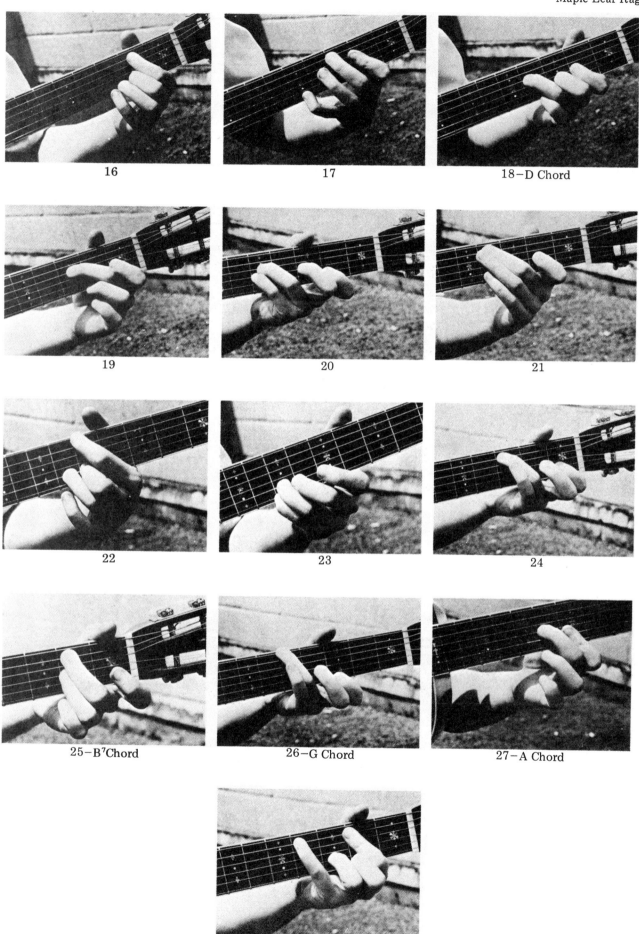

16

17

18—D Chord

19

20

21

22

23

24

25—B⁷Chord

26—G Chord

27—A Chord

28

Maple Leaf Rag

Red Pepper Rag

This arrangement for *Red Pepper Rag* was taken note-for-note from a very patient pianist from Berkeley, California. I had to develop a new tuning in order to keep the flavor of the original as well as to be able to play all the necessary counterpoint lines. The result is that the guitar is tuned: C G D G B E.

This is a very convenient tuning as it allows us to modulate from the key of C to the key of G and still keep an alternating bass. There are four sections to this rag as well as an introduction and bridge. The running order is: first section played twice, then second section played twice, first again played once, bridge, third section played twice and finally the fourth section played twice.

This fingering is quite tricky and you will find it difficult to play this at the proper speed. Practicing every day will help you develop the speed. Don't be discouraged if it takes you a long time to master this arrangement. I devised it several years ago and still cannot play it without making an error or two or three.

I have recorded this on my Transatlantic disc *Yazoo Basin Boogie*.

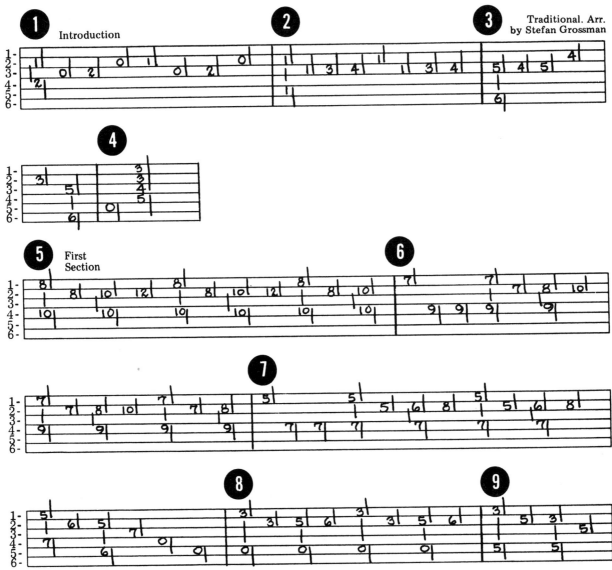

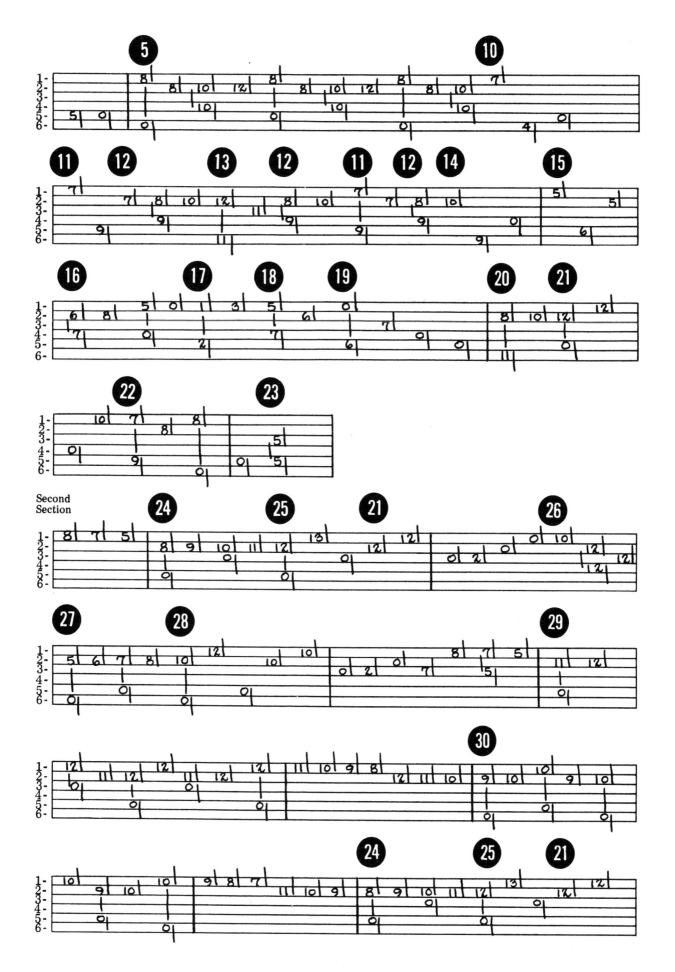

Red Pepper Rag

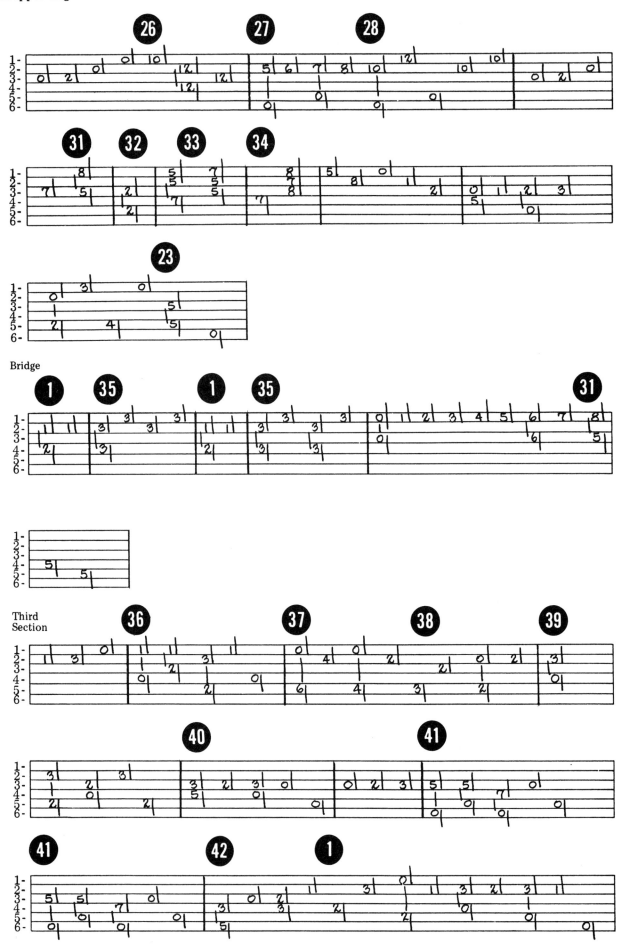

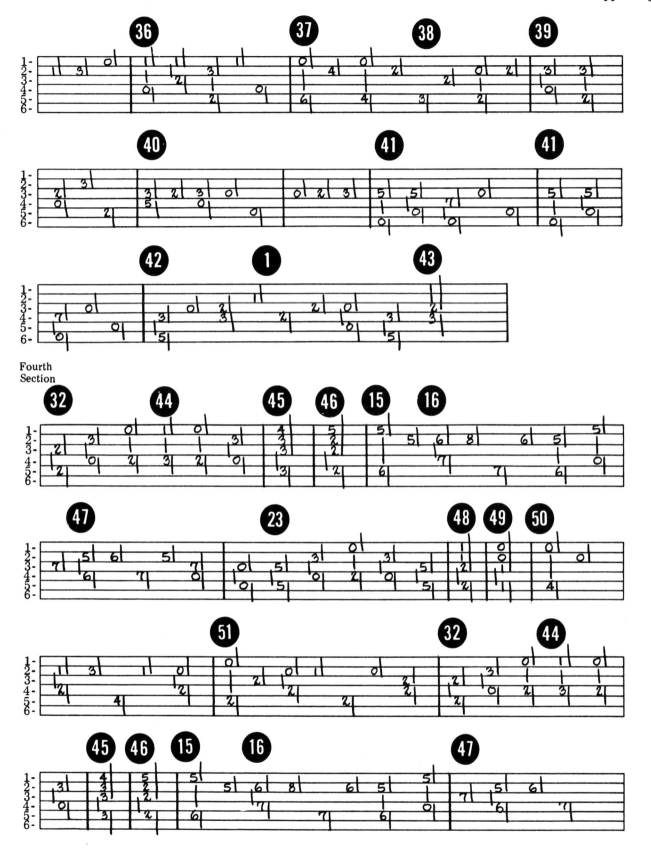

Red Pepper Rag

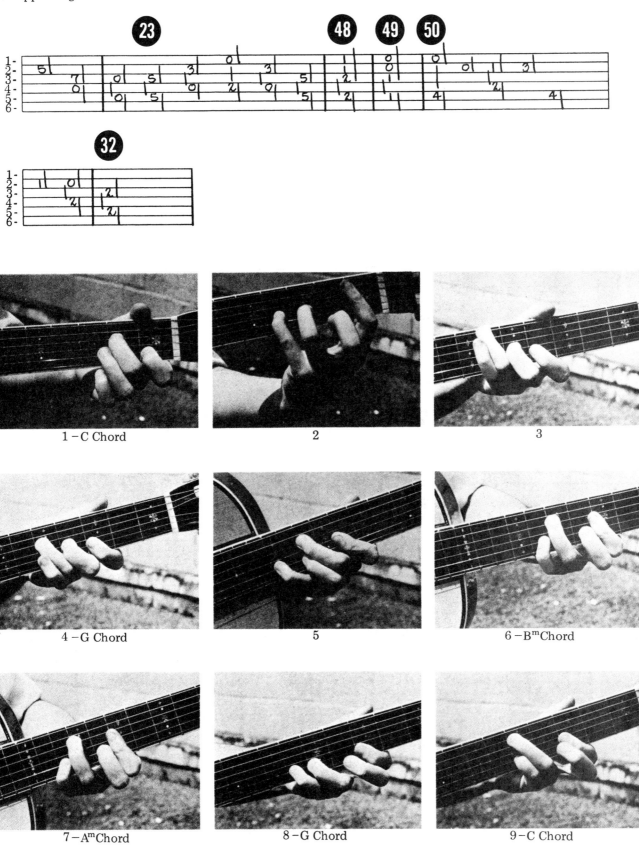

1 – C Chord

2

3

4 – G Chord

5

6 – B^m Chord

7 – A^m Chord

8 – G Chord

9 – C Chord

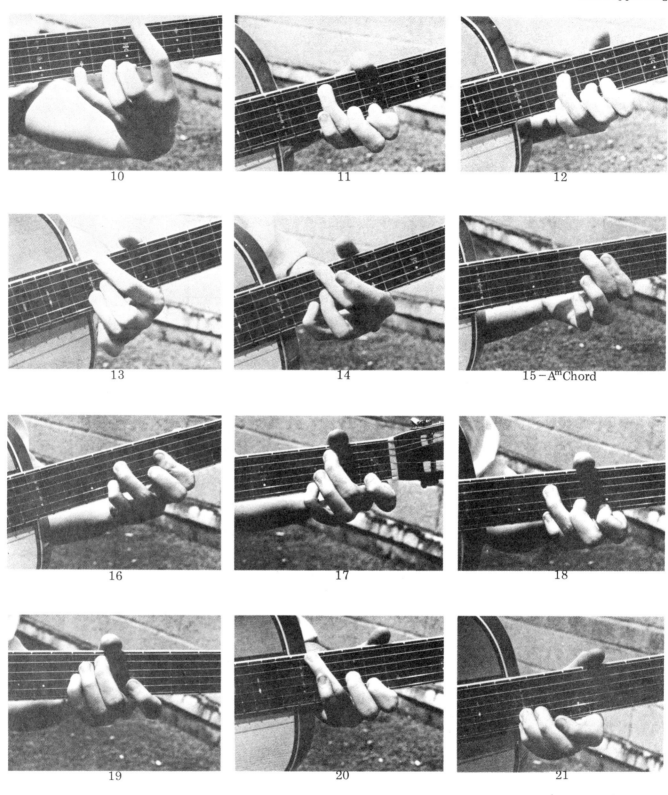

10

11

12

13

14

15 – A^m Chord

16

17

18

19

20

21

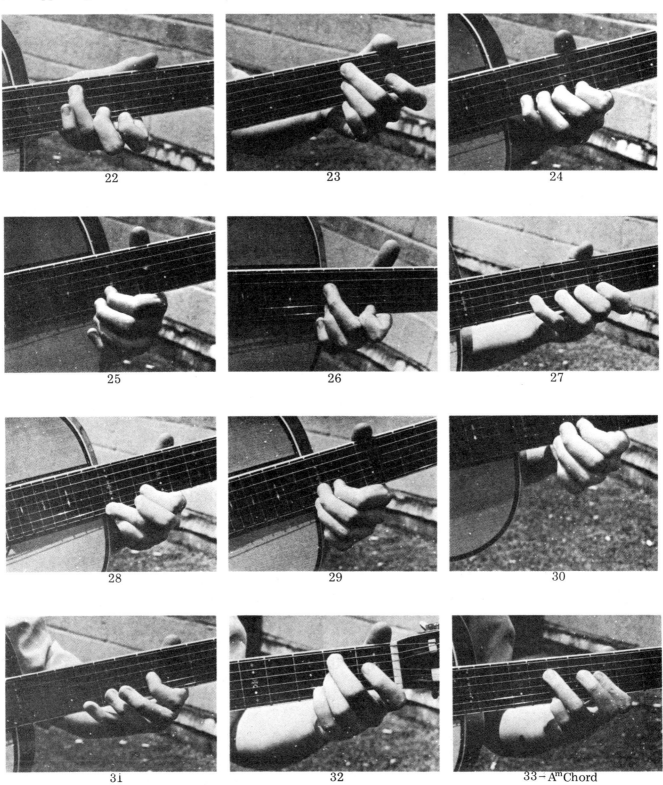

22

23

24

25

26

27

28

29

30

3i

32

33 – A^m Chord

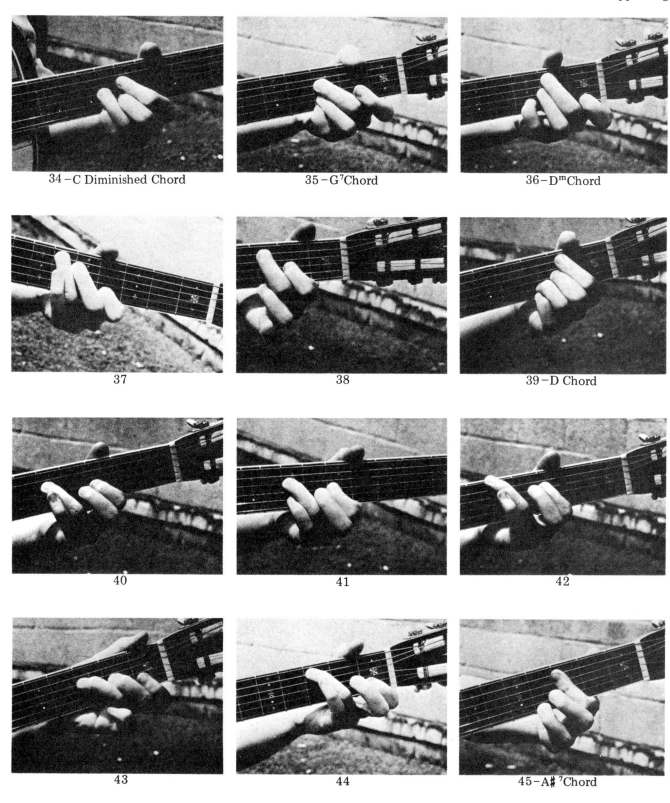

34 – C Diminished Chord

35 – G⁷ Chord

36 – Dᵐ Chord

37

38

39 – D Chord

40

41

42

43

44

45 – A♯⁷ Chord

Red Pepper Rag

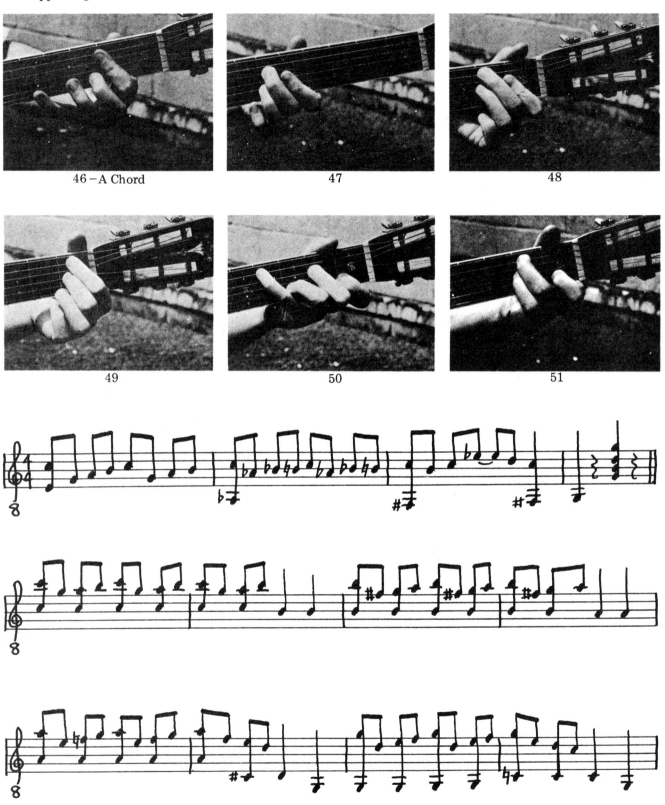

46 – A Chord   47   48

49   50   51

Red Pepper Rag

Ragtime Songs

The Old Piano Roll Blues

This is that old barber-shop quartet favorite that should be familiar to you. Many of my guitarist friends have arranged this piece and I have picked Ric Schoenberg's to transcribe. His is full of counterpoint lines and should prove fun for you to play.

It is played in regular tuning to the key of C. One essential phrase is repeated over and over with variations. You should find this tune pretty easy.

You can get a recording of this by writing to Black Patty Tape Service.

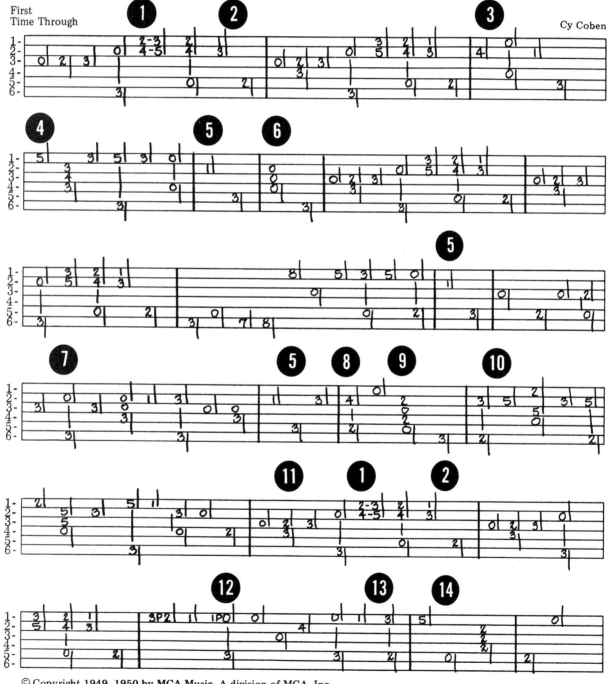

The Old Piano Roll Blues

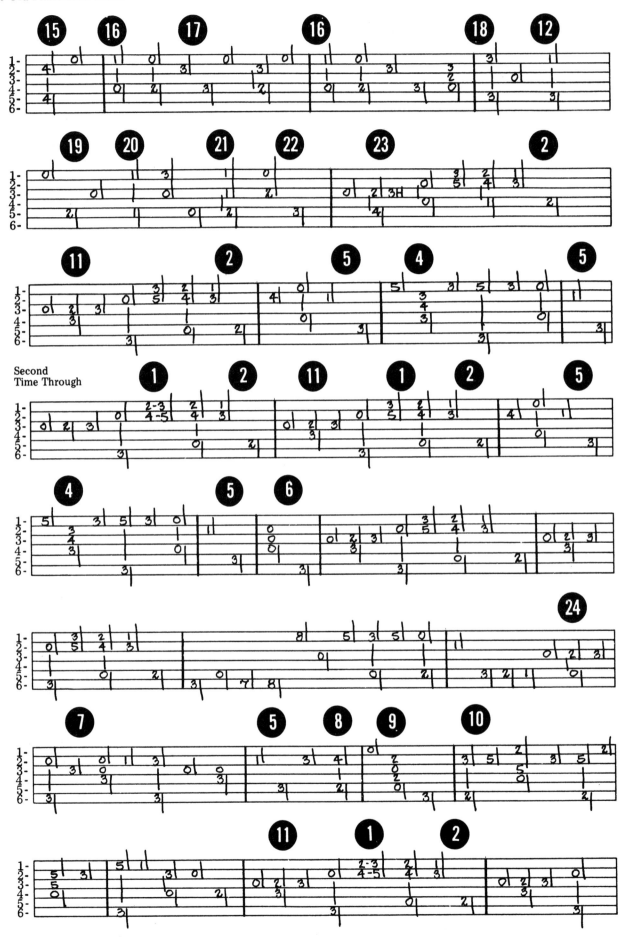

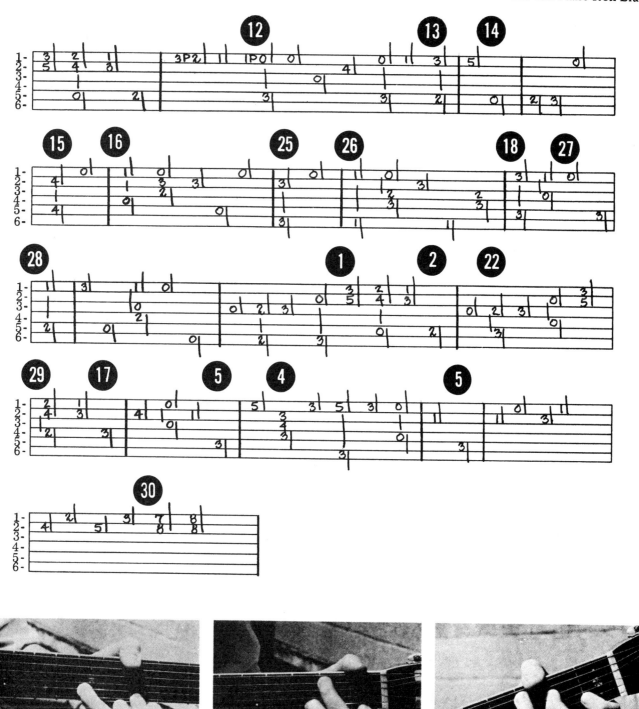

1

2 – C⁷ Chord

3 – C Chord

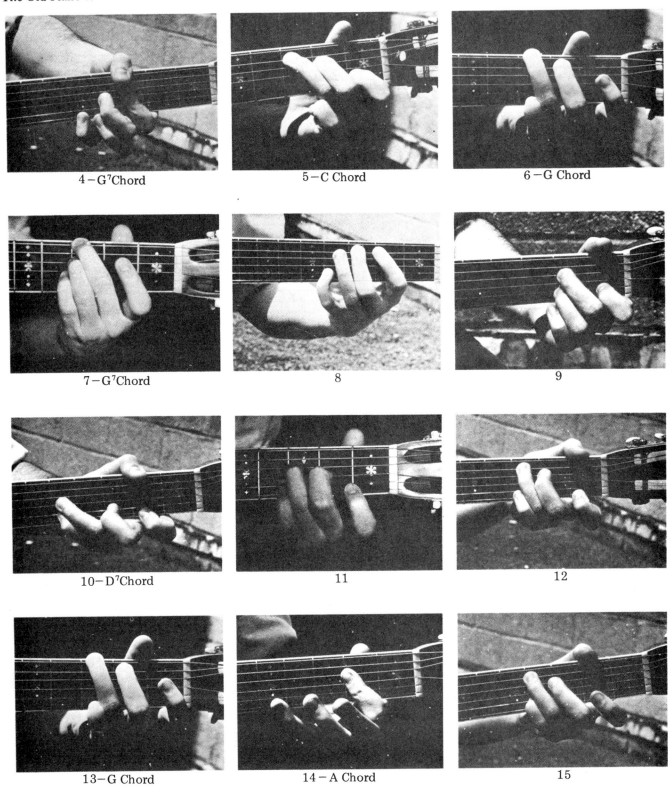

4 — G⁷ Chord

5 — C Chord

6 — G Chord

7 — G⁷ Chord

8

9

10 — D⁷ Chord

11

12

13 — G Chord

14 — A Chord

15

16—D^mChord   17   18—C Chord

19   20   21

22   23   24

25—G Chord   26—F Chord   27

28   29   30

The Old Piano Roll Blues

The Old Piano Roll Blues

New Sounds

Roberta

Roberta was the first instrumental I composed. It has its roots in country blues and ragtime sounds yet sounds much different than either style. It is played in the key of A in a regular tuning. Instead of using a rigid counterpoint line I incorporated bass and middle registered figures to over-lay over a treble melody line. One cannot exist without the other and this is what makes this tune interesting. It has a flowing feel somewhat reminiscent of the playing of Tommy Johnson but this is a far cry from a country blues. The harmonic structure and tonality are quite modern and people have said it crosses from the Mississippi to Bach. This is quite a wide range and I hope that you enjoy it.

I have recorded this on *Aunt Molly's Murray Farm* (Kicking Mule Records, Sonet Records). Since composing this piece I have written many more that can be heard on various records that I have done.

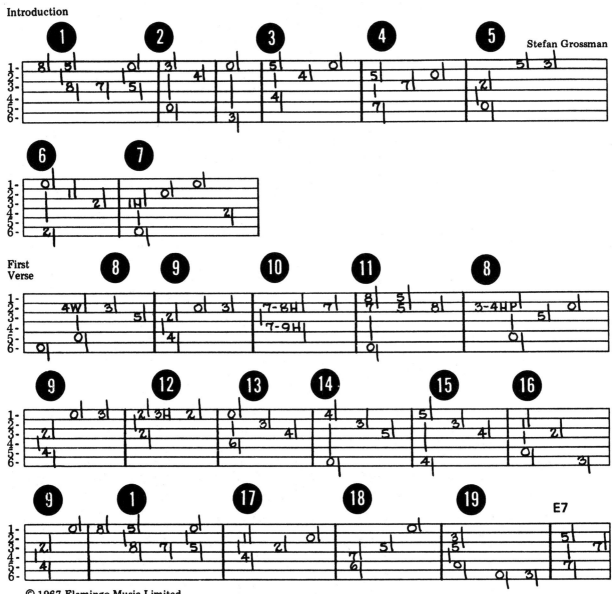

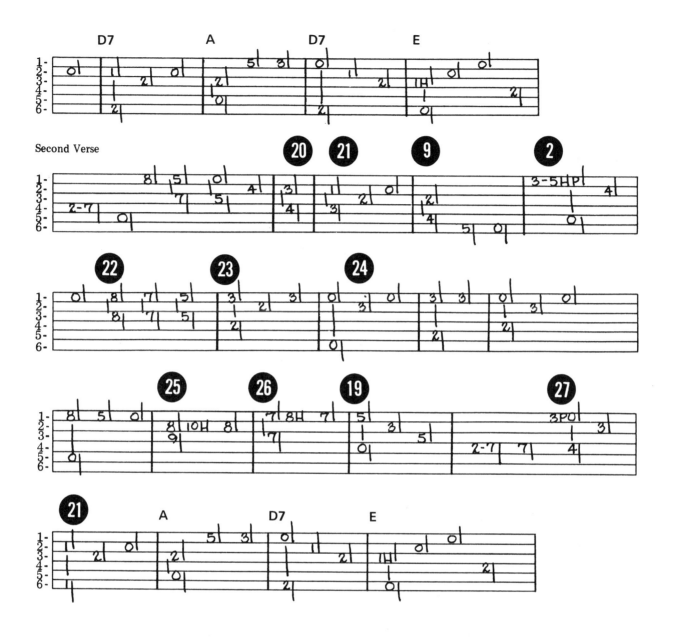

Second Verse

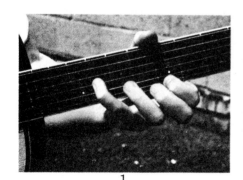

1

2

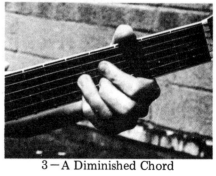

3 — A Diminished Chord

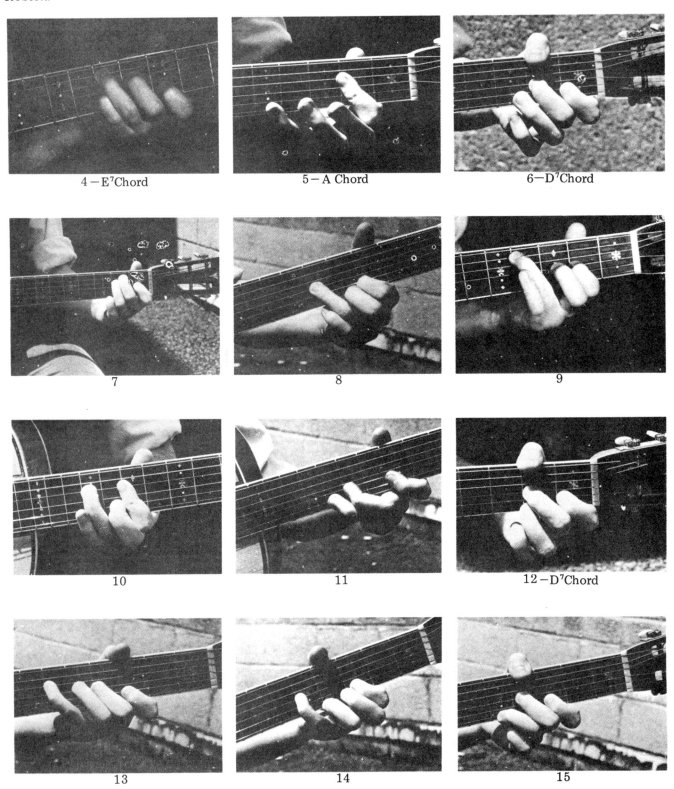

4 — E⁷ Chord

5 — A Chord

6 — D⁷ Chord

7

8

9

10

11

12 — D⁷ Chord

13

14

15

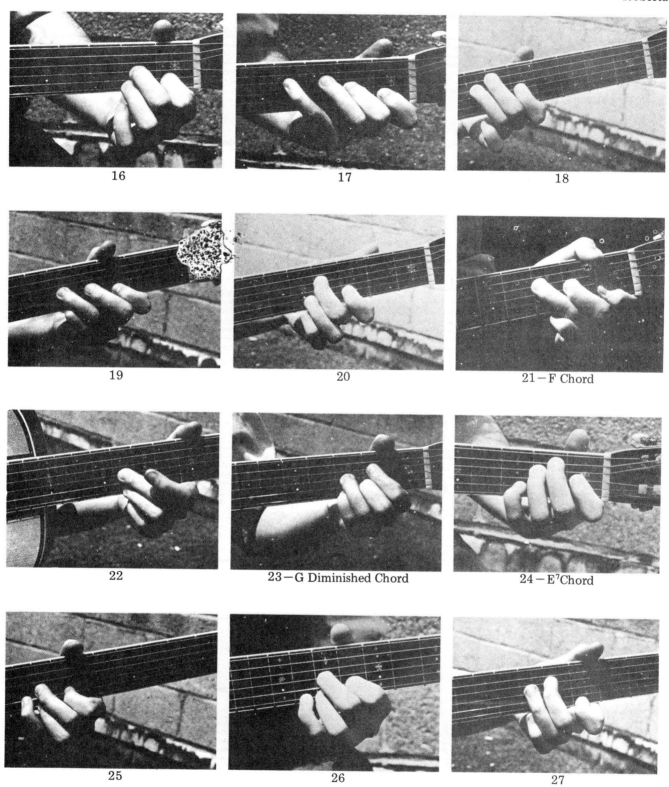

16

17

18

19

20

21 — F Chord

22

23 — G Diminished Chord

24 — E⁷ Chord

25

26

27

Roberta

Discography

I have recorded the following discs that might be of interest to you:

Aunt Molly's Murray Farm (Kicking Mule Records [American release],
        Sonet Records [European release])
The Gramercy Park Sheik (Kicking Mule Records [American release],
        Sonet Records [European release])
Crosscurrents (Cotillion SD9007)
Yazoo Basin Boogie (Transatlantic, Kicking Mule Records)

There are many wonderful contemporary guitarists who have recorded and unfortunately many who have not yet had this opportunity. You might find some of the following records of interest. Many of these have been issued in America and Europe but under different company names.

Bert Jansch:	*Birthday Blues*	Transatlantic 179
	Nicola	Transatlantic 157
	Jack Orion	Transatlantic 143
Bert Jansch and John Renbourn:		
	Bert and John	Transatlantic 144
John Renbourn:	*Sir John Alot Of . .*	Transatlantic 167
Martin Carthy:	*Two Came By*	Fontana 5477
	Byker Hill	Fontana 5434
	Second Album	Fontana 5362
Gordon Giltrap:	*Portrait*	Transatlantic 202
Ralph McTell:	*Spiral Staircase*	Transatlantic 177
Pat Kilroy:	*Light of Day*	Elektra 7311
Dave Laibman and Eric Schoenberg:		
	Ragtime Guitar	Folkways 3528

Records by Davy Graham, Jack Elliot, John Koerner, and John Fahey are also recommended.

Modern Ragtime guitar has not been over-recorded but I think you will find Blind Blake, Big Bill Broonzy, Reverand Gary Davis, Blind Boy Fuller and many other old bluesmen valuable to listen to. My Oak book *Ragtime Blues Guitarists* presents a study of these styles.

To order European records, you can write to: Collets Record Shop
                                      70 New Oxford Street
                                      London, England

All of the songs in this collection have been put on a tape that can be obtained from: Black Patty Tape Service
                    c/o Grossman
                    32 Gramercy Park South
                    New York City, 10003, New York
                    U.S.A.

The Tablature System

I began to play music at an early age. The formality and coldness of the teaching methods as well as the dull material brought a quick end to my interest. The printed music page seemed a strange and difficult language to master. Anyway, who was interested in *Autumn Leaves* or *Tea For Two*? The songs had no personal appeal for me. Five years later I once again picked up a guitar and started to play. This time I wisely shied away from organized music theory. Sounds from my head found their way to the guitar. I concentrated on playing and not on learning about sharps, flats, time signatures, key changes and chord structures. I didn't want to be cramped by words.

A few months after that, I found myself sitting in front of Rev. Gary Davis, learning how to play from him.

For two years I concentrated on the many styles Rev. Davis patiently taught me. I spent hours up at his house breathing in thick cigar smoke, eating Mrs. Davis' cooking and learning incredible songs. It was during this time that I devised a method for writing down the songs Rev. Davis was teaching me. I needed this so that I could learn more in a lesson and remember it all. So instead of two songs a day I was able to absorb five. The system I developed showed only the fret positions of the strings. The sound, rhythm, and accent of the piece was all in my head. My system depended on hearing the song. The chord positions were drawn or rather scribbled out so that no fingering problems would arise.

The tablature presented here is a culmination of the system developed at Rev. Davis' house. Instead of sketches I have photographs of hand positions. The system still relies on hearing the piece of music. All of the items presented here are available either on record or on tape. The sources are all listed before each song and in the discography at the end of each volume.

Tablature is intended for those people who want to learn how to play first and learn theory second. Tablature can help you to find the notes, while the records can give you the feel of a song. Then it's up to you to put the song together. Your fingers and your touch are your own. These are unique and will produce your own sound no matter how hard you try to imitate.

Now for the tablature:

Each space indicates a string:

1 means the high E
2 means the B (or second string)
3 means the G string
4 means the D string
5 means the A string
6 means the low E string

A number on this space indicates the fretted position. A *zero* would mean open string. The number *1* indicates the first fret of that string. (Note the diagram below.) The *zero* on the second string indicates that the open second string should be played. The *1* placed on the third string's space indicates first fret on the third string. Likewise *4* placed on the fourth string's space indicates fourth fret of the fourth string.

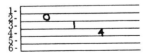

All the volumes of this series are concerned with fingerpicking guitar styles. These are generally played with the thumb, index and middle fingers of the right hand (presuming that you are right-handed). To indicate which finger to use, flags are placed next to the numbers that show fretted positions. A flag down means that the thumb strikes the note. If the flag is up then your index or middle finger (whichever you prefer) should strike the note. The choice will clarify itself when playing a song up to tempo.

The diagram below shows an open sixth string played with the thumb and the second fret of the third string played with the index finger.

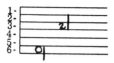

In most cases the thumb will play an alternating bass usually on the top three bass strings. The index and middle finger will play notes on the first, second and third strings. But again these aren't rules and there are many exceptions.

In fingerpicking there are two choices. Either we pinch two notes together or we don't (also called a pluck in some books). A pinch is shown by connecting the two notes with a line. A variation of this comes when two treble notes are pinched with a bass note.

In the above example we have from left to right the following: first the open sixth string is played by the thumb. Next the first fret of the sixth string is pinched together with the third fret of the third string. The sixth string is plucked by the thumb and the third by the index finger. Next the thumb strikes the third fret of the fourth string. This is similar to an alternating bass pattern. The next notes are the first fret sixth string played by the thumb. This is pinched with two notes in the treble. The index and middle finger strike the first fret first string and the third fret second string. The next note is the index finger hitting the first fret second string. Lastly we have the bass note played with the thumb on the third fret fourth string.

In blues many times the notes are not decisively played. The tablature makes this clear.

In the first case the thumb hits the open sixth string but the second fret on the fifth string also sounds. This is done simply by playing harder on the sixth string. The force will make the fifth string vibrate. This technique is done in the bass as well as treble section of a song. Next we see an arrow. This indicates a brush. The direction is found in the arrowhead. If pointed up, the hand brushes up towards the sixth string. If down, the hand brushes down to the first string. The amount of strings to be affected are shown by the length of the arrow. For instance the next group of notes shows a brush up towards the sixth string of the open first, open second and first fret third string. Next is the bass open sixth string with the vibrating fifth. Next is an arrow up. Again we brush up towards the sixth string but this time the second fret of the fourth string vibrates and sounds. It is not hit but is affected by the other three notes. This effect is gotten by dampening the strings with your right hand palm or by an upward stroke of the right hand. This sound is difficult to explain. But in many pieces you can hear notes sounding yet you know distinctly that they are not being hit. This is in the nature of the guitar. By hitting one note it will set other notes to sound. The last notes in this example are a brush down to the first string of the open first, open second, and first fret third string.

Now let's look at the same example with the chord letter and chord picture added. The first indicates what chord it is. The circled number indicates which photograph this fingering corresponds to.

2— E Chord

In order to keep the tablature from being cluttered up with circles I did not include them in a repeated segment of a piece. I presume you will remember the positions. The chords are given where I think helpful. Some finger positions have involved chord designations. Instead of complicating the song with this additional information I let the photographs tell you what is needed. Once you have learned the music you can go back and learn the theory.

There are certain effects used in blues guitar that are also symbolized in the tablature. Here are some examples; explanations follow.

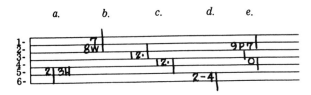

a. The hammer-on. Here the fret hammered is placed after the flag. In this case the second fret is played by the thumb and then the third fret is hammered. This is all done in one continuous motion and produces a single sound.

b. The wham or slurred note. This is designated by a "w". In this case the eighth fret second string is whammed and played with the seventh fret first string. Both notes are played with index and middle fingers respectively.

c. The harmonic. This is symbolized by a dot (•). The two notes are both harmonics. The first is the twelfth fret third string played by index finger. The next is the twelfth fret fourth string hit by the thumb.

d. The slide. This is shown by a dash (—). This reads: second fret sixth string slides to fourth fret sixth string. These notes are struck by the thumb.

e. The pull off. This shows the note pulled off and what remains. The letter "P" designates this effect. The last note reads: ninth fret second string is pulled off against the seventh fret second string. Also we are pinching the open fourth string with our thumb.

This sounds wordy and complicated. But once you become familiar with the tablature it will all become very simple and automatic. All of my students end up sight-reading the tablature. The photos will illuminate the positions in these effects. As for tonality and accent, these are for you to hear in the originals.

—Peace,
Stefan Grossman

The Music System

The music notation in this book is as simple and clear as we could make it. If you don't know how to read it, this is a very good place to learn. This traditional European notation does not always work perfectly, but it's very much worth knowing.

The basic rhythmic idea is steady, even beats with regular accents. "HUP, two, three, four, HUP, two, three, four, HUP, two, three, four, HUP, two, three, four," or Indian war drums in old movies: "BOOM boom boom boom BOOM boom boom boom BOOM boom boom boom BOOM boom boom boom." In music notation, it would look like this:

A beautiful melody from Beethoven's Ninth Symphony has a similar rhythm:

Frau-de, schö-ne göt-ter-fun-ken Toch-ter aus E -ly - si-um,

The drums had an actual accent (>) on the first beat of every four. The Beethoven theme does not, but we still feel it.

A phrase sometimes starts before or after the first beat of a measure:

I - wish I was- in the land of cot -ton.

(That is one important difference between the tablature and the music notation in this collection.)

The shape of a note tells how long it lasts. When a quarter-note (♩) takes one beat, then a half-note (♩) takes two beats, a whole-note (○) takes four beats, an eighth-note (♪) takes half a beat, and a sixteenth-note (♪) takes a quarter of a beat. A dot after a note makes it last 50% longer. A dotted half note (♩.) takes three beats; a dotted quarter-note takes one-and-a-half beats (♩.). A grace note (♪) is considered to take no time at all.

We could let half-noted (♩) or eighth notes (♪) or anything else stand for beats.

I- wish I was- in the land of cot -ton.

But quarter-notes are generally used for this. That is the meaning of the bottom number in a key signature like $\frac{4}{4}$.

The top number tells how many beats in an accented group. Two-beat measures:

Ha - vah__ Na-gi - lah, Ha - vah __ Na-gi-lah, Ha -vah ___Na-gi-lah,

ve - nis ___ m' - chah.

The triplet of eighth notes lasts for one whole beat, not one and-a-half beats, as three regular eighth notes would. We don't have special note-shapes for one-third or a quarter-note.

However, if you want most of the beats in a song to be divided into threes, you can call the divisions "beats:"

When John- ny comes mar 3 -ching home 3 a -gain 3 hur rah! - hur rah!

$\frac{6}{8}$ does not mean the same thing as $\frac{3}{4}$.

Oh, say, can you see ?

$\frac{3}{4}$ time and $\frac{6}{8}$ time can be compared in two different ways:

Comparing beat for beat:

Comparing measure for measure;

$\frac{6}{8}$ can also be slow:

A - las, my love, _you do me wrong_ To cast me off__ dis-cour-teous-ly,

It still means only two real beats to the measure.

Rock 'n' roll records of the 1950's, especially the slow ones, usually had four beats to a measure, divided into triplets.

There is also a $\frac{9}{8}$ time, three beats to the measure, divided into triplets:

On top of Old Smo-ky, — all co-vered with snow. — I lost my true

lo-ver — by cour -ting too slow.

(This song is sometimes sung in $\frac{12}{8}$, four beats to a measure.)

The blues rhythms in this book most often have two notes to the beat. Usually the first of the two is played somewhat longer, but we write plain eighth-notes, except when real triplets are felt. Some people write this "swing rhythm" as a dotted rhythm (♫ ♫ ♫ ♫).

You take the high road , and I take the low road ,

Most of the music in this collection is in $\frac{4}{4}$ or $\frac{12}{8}$.

Pitch is shown by placing a note somewhere on a five-line "staff" (or its higher or lower extension), sometimes adjusting higher ("sharp", ♯) or lower ("flat", ♭).

Joy to the world! The Lord is come! Let Earth re-ceive her King!

This example does not use sharp or flat signs, because it happens to be written at a general pitch level, or key, that on the piano keyboard uses only white notes, no black notes. Our notation is based a lot on the piano keyboard, although musically this key sounds just like the other keys involving some white and some black notes.

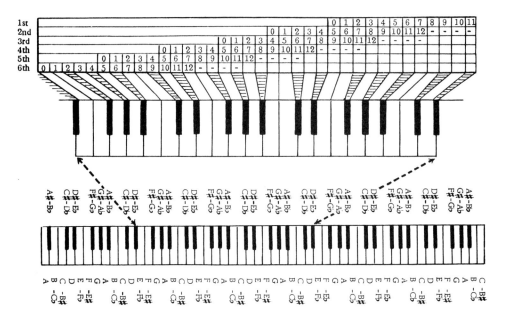

The steps between the white notes are not all the same size. The steps from F to E ("the Lord" in the last musical example) and from B to C ("Joy to" and "her King") are "half-steps" (one guitar fret). The other steps are "whole-steps" (two frets). The steps between white notes and neighboring black notes are half-steps.

Notice how the highest note in the last song sounds like the lowest note. They are both called C; they are an "octave" apart. When higher and lower voices sing music together in "unison", they generally sing an octave apart. The C major scale, or any other scale, involves not only the eight notes of one octave but also the same notes in all other octaves.

The interval from B to F is a diminished fifth. The other fifths in the scale are "perfect" fifths. There is always one diminished fifth in any major scale, and it leans very hard on the tonic.

The figure 8 under the treble clef in guitar music means that the sound is an octave lower than written.

The perfect fifths in the scale are very harmonious and contented, not leaning especially on anything. However, they all become harmonically involved with either or both of the two crucial notes of the diminished fifth. As a result, everything in the C major scale eventually lends its harmonic support to the tonic note C.

If we raise F to F♯, we have a perfect fifth, B♮ - F♯, but at the same time the old perfect fifth, F♮ - C♮, becomes a diminished fifth F♯ - C♮. This one change completely shifts the balance of power to the note G, the new tonic in a G-major scale with the same harmonic pattern of half-steps and whole-steps, and the same possibilities, problems, harmonies, and relations, as we had in the C-major scale, only this time a perfect fifth higher, or a perfect fourth lower.

Returning temporarily to the key of C, with once again the diminished fifth from B to F♮, if we lower the B to a B♭, we get again a perfect fifth, and once again we get a new diminished fifth (E♮ to B♭), this time replacing the perfect fifth E♮ - B♮. Now the scale is in F major.

These key changes can go on forever. For instance from F major we could change E♮ to E♭ and arrive in B♭ major. Or from G major we could change C♮ to C♯ and arrive in D major.

A song can also be in one key, A for example, but use some or all of the notes from another key, C major for example, or G major, F major, B major ... this gives a different quality to the music, since the diminished fifth now leads somewhere else than to the tonic. In such "model" scales, the tonic is established more by the writing than by the harmonic situation built into the scale. The power in such music is not as clearly concentrated on the tonic note as it is in the "Major Mode".

The sharps or flats traditionally belonging to a key are generally given at the beginning of each staff. They apply automatically to all such notes in the music unless they are altered by sharps, flats, or naturals in the text, called accidentals.

A scale is called major or minor according to the pitch of the third scale note. A major third (four half-steps) sounds happier than a minor third (three half-steps). A minor scale (A-minor for example) traditionally uses the key signature of the third (C♮ in this case), whether the music uses the actual notes of C major, F major, or G major (or most likely a mixture of any or all of these with notes from the A-major scale.) Blues are generally somewhere between major and minor, so in this collection we use the traditional key signature of the major key with accidentals in the text. Here is a chart of traditional key signatures for major and minor keys.

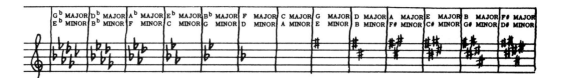

| G♭ MAJOR
E♭ MINOR | D♭ MAJOR
B♭ MINOR | A♭ MAJOR
F MINOR | E♭ MAJOR
C MINOR | B♭ MAJOR
G MINOR | F MAJOR
D MINOR | C MAJOR
A MINOR | G MAJOR
E MINOR | D MAJOR
B MINOR | A MAJOR
F♯ MINOR | E MAJOR
C♯ MINOR | B MAJOR
G♯ MINOR | F♯ MAJOR
D♯ MINOR |

Natural-signs are implied where there are no sharps or flats. Notice the interval of a diminished fifth between the last ♯ or ♭ and the natural-note which will become ♯ or ♭ in the next key (the key a perfect fifth higher or lower). This is the same diminished fifth that we discussed before.

Notice also that in some of the more difficult-looking keys we use E♯ and B♯, which are played the same as F♮ and C♮. In the music in the book you will also see F✕ (F double-sharp), played like G♮. The sign F♮♯ means the same as F♯, and is used in order to be distinct from F✕.

We have already talked about ties between two notes of the same pitch, sounding as a single longer pitch.

We use the same curved line between two different notes as a "slur", meaning that the second note is not plucked but rather hammered on or pulled off.

The curved line going from a note and ending nowhere in particular means that the note connects past the next note to some other note farther on.

Of course, about half of the notes in this music do this anyway. This sign is used where there might otherwise be a misunderstanding.

A short straight line between two notes means a slide. With a slur mark the second note again is not plucked. Two special guitar symbols (w, ↓) are explained with the tablature.

The notation used in this collection is in some ways simpler than the standard method of the present day. It gives all of the same information, but in a way that is especially designed to encourage the beginning reader. People familiar with standard notation will have no trouble reading this. However, someone who learns to read from this collection may have a little bit of trouble reading standard publications. For instance, the standard method lets an accidental (♯, ♭, or ♮) extend its meaning until the next bar line. In using accidental more generously, I am returning to the standard practice of the period before the nineteenth century. If a beginner has any trouble, there are plenty of books everywhere explaining the standard practice of today in great detail.

—Larry Leitch